MEDIA, FEMINISM, CULTURAL STUDIES

FROM CRESCENT MOON PUBLISHING

Arseny Tarkovsky: *Life, Life: Selected Poems*
translated by Virginia Rounding

Stepping Forward: Essays, Lectures and Interviews
by Wolfgang Iser

Wild Zones: Pornography, Art and Feminism
by Kelly Ives

Global Media Warning: Explorations of Radio, Television and the Press
by Oliver Whitehorne

'Cosmo Woman': The World of Women's Magazines
by Oliver Whitehorne

Andrea Dworkin
by Jeremy Mark Robinson

Cixous, Irigaray, Kristeva: The Jouissance *of French Feminism*
by Kelly Ives

Sex in Art: Pornography and Pleasure in Painting and Sculpture
by Cassidy Hughes

The Erotic Object: Sexuality in Sculpture From Prehistory to the Present Day
by Susan Quinnell

Women in Pop Music
by Helen Challis

Detonation Britain: Nuclear War in the Uk
by Jeremy Mark Robinson

Julia Kristeva: Art, Love, Melancholy, Philosophy, Semiotics and Psychoanalysis
by Kelly Ives

Luce Irigaray: Lips, Kissing, and the Politics of Sexual Difference
by Kelly Ives

THE BEAST

WALERIAN BOROWCZYK

The Beast

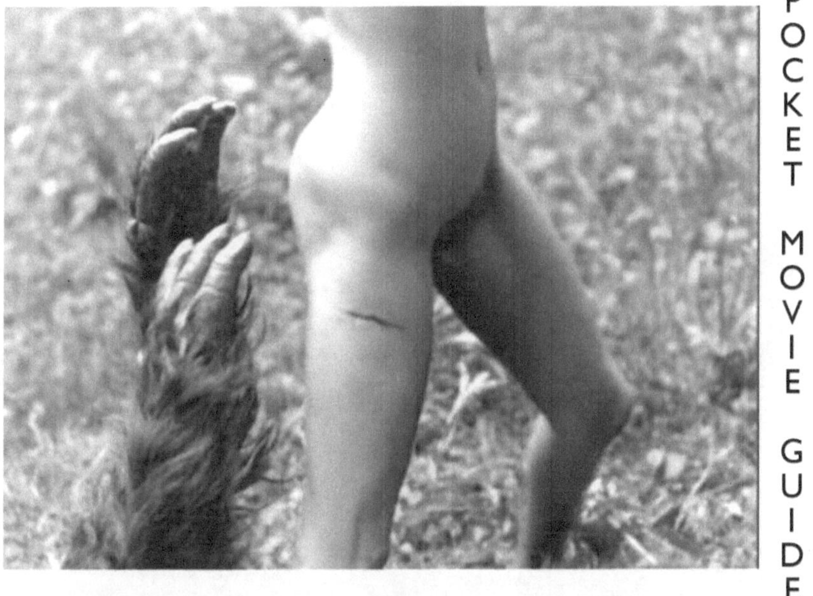

POCKET MOVIE GUIDE

Walerian Borowczyk

An Erotic Fairy Tale

Jeremy Mark Robinson

CRESCENT MOON

First published 2013.

Printed and bound in the U.S.A.
Set in Rotis Serif 9 on 14pt, and Gill Sans Light display.
Designed by Radiance Graphics.

British Library Cataloguing in Publication data available for this title.

ISBN-13 9781861714244 (Pbk)

Crescent Moon Publishing
P.O. Box 1312
Maidstone, Kent
ME14 5XU, Great Britain
www.crmoon.com

CONTENTS

Acknowledgements 8
Illustrations 11

1 The Cinema of Walerian Borowczyk 15
Illustrations 57
2 *The Beast* 87

Appendices
Quotes By Walerian Borowczyk 133
Other Versions of Beauty and the Beast 135
A Note On Fairy Tales 144
Filmography 157
Bibliography 162

ACKNOWLEDGEMENTS

To the copyright holders of the illustrations.
To authors quoted and their publishers.

PICTURE CREDITS

Argos Films. Pagan. Cult Epics. Severin Films. Naja Films. Palace Video. New Horizon. Gaumont/ Columbia. C.A.V. Distribution. Nouveaux Pictures. New Line Cinema. Sara Distribution. Jupiter Communications. CDF Films. Lisa Film. Top Video.

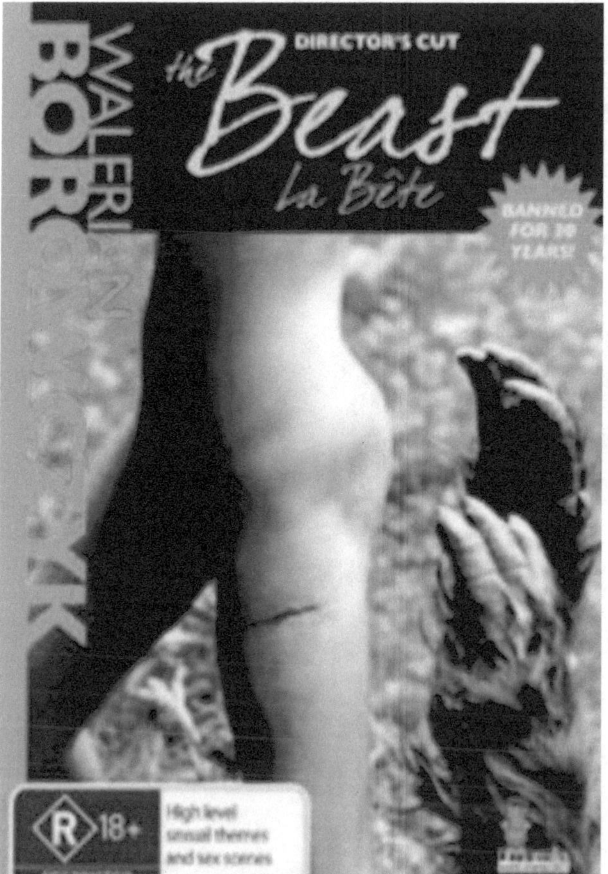
DIRECTOR'S CUT
the Beast
La Bête
BANNED FOR 30 YEARS!
R 18+
High level sexual themes and sex scenes
RESTRICTED

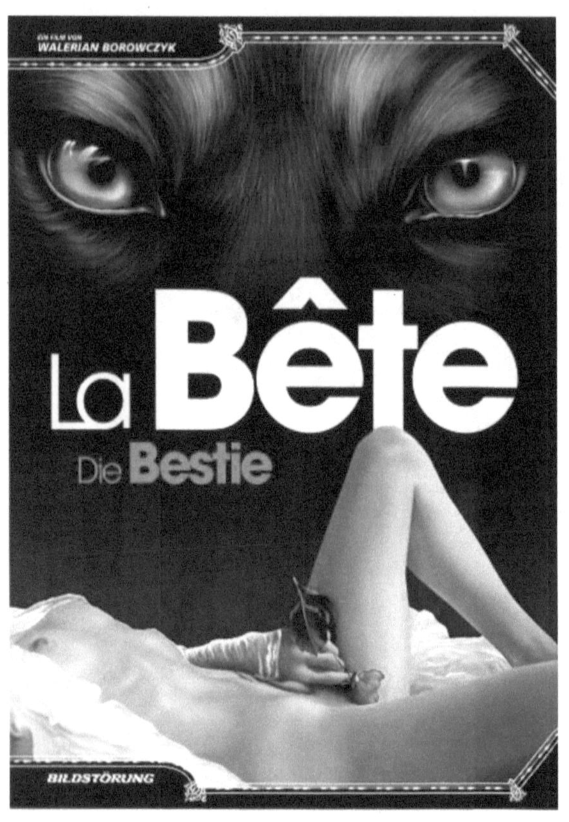
EIN FILM VON
WALERIAN BOROWCZYK
La Bête
Die Bestie
BILDSTÖRUNG

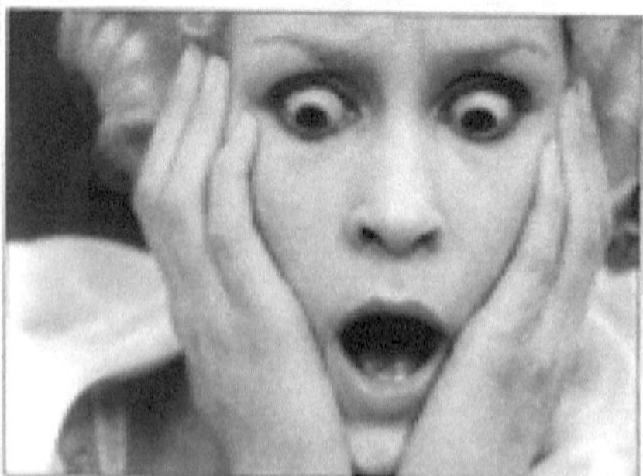
the
Walerian Borowczyk
collection
THE BEAST
GOTO
ISLAND OF LOVE
LOVE RITES

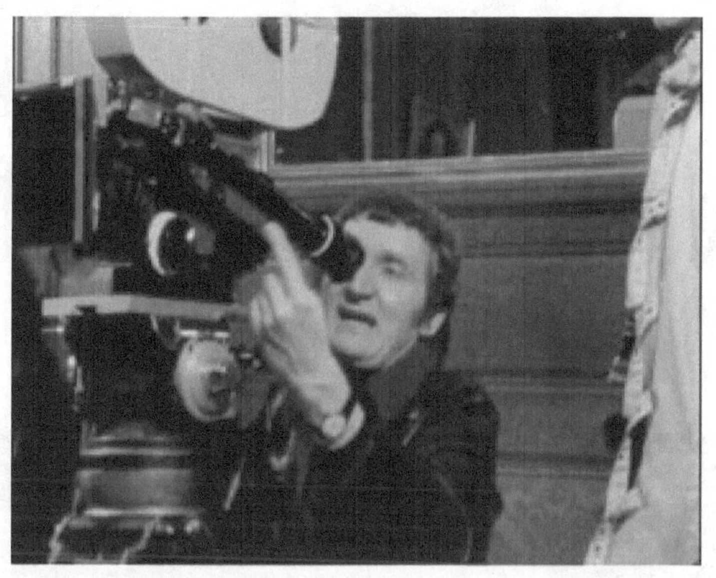

Walerian Borowczyk directing The Beast

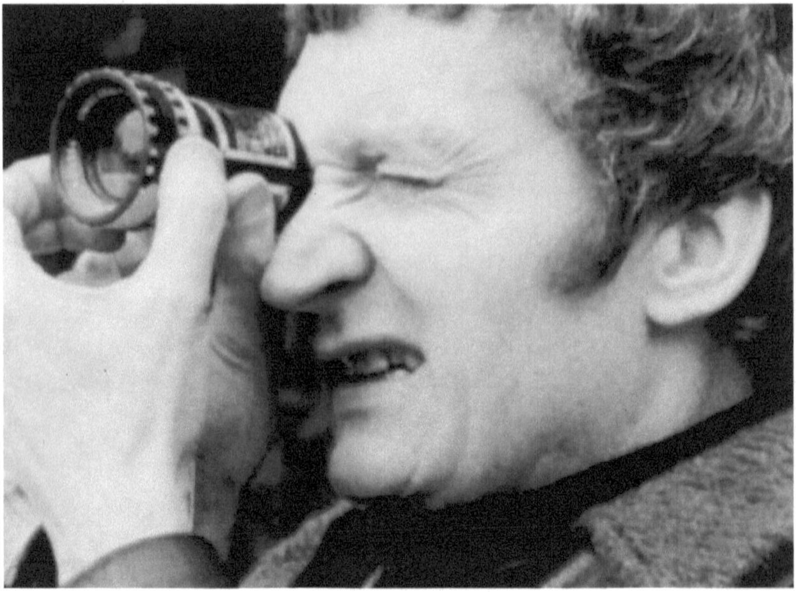

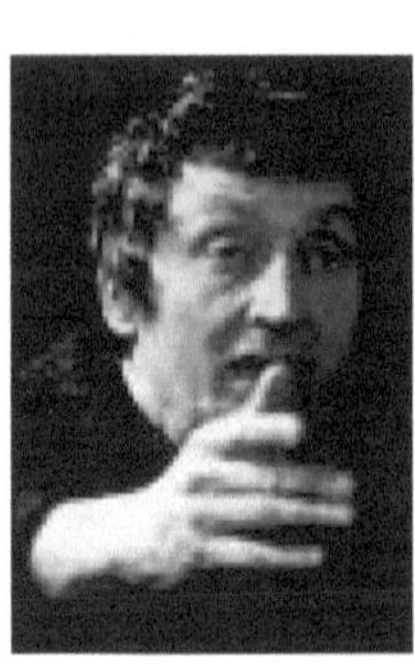

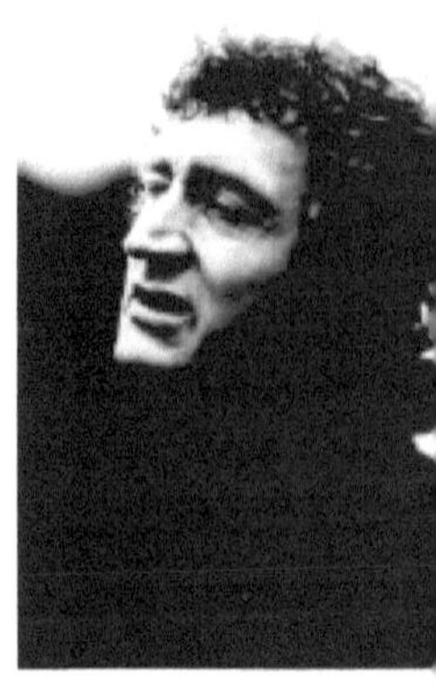

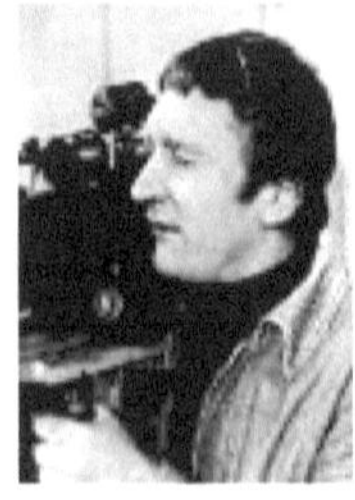

I

THE CINEMA OF WALERIAN BOROWCZYK

Eroticism, sex, is one of the most moral parts of life. Eroticism does not kill, exterminate, encourage evil, lead to crime. On the contrary, it makes people gentler, brings joy, gives fulfilment, leads to selfless pleasure.

Walerian Borowczyk[1]

Walerian Borowczyk (known as 'Boro') is one of cinema's one-offs. Quite simply, there is no filmmaker quite like Borowczyk. Borowczyk's movies have an extraordinary, magical quality. They reach a place very rare in contemporary cinema, and are quite unlike the pictures of any other *auteur*. Borowczyk's films create their own space, with imagery, sounds and music of a really exceptional power.

Goto: Island of Love was the first Walerian Borowczyk film that made a big impression on audiences and critics, winning a number of prizes. I first saw *Goto; Island of Love* in 1982, at Bournemouth Film School, when we watched 16mm prints as part of our film history course. You could see there was an astonishing vision at work here. I remember above all the creation of a

1 Interview with Andrzej Markowski, *Kino*, 4, 1975.

visceral, idiosyncratic and original world.

If I had to single out some movies, I'd cite *Blanche, Immoral Tales, Behind Convent Walls, The Beast* and *Goto*, for their painterly sense, the use of props and costumes, and the incredible attention to detail. Very sophisticated, mysterious, poetic. Not forgetting the acute awareness of the history of religion and literature. Walerian Borowczyk produced some of the most memorable images in European cinema, the equal of Ingmar Bergman, Sergei Paradjanov or Andrei Tarkovsky.

I reckon there's one absolute Walerian Borowczyk masterpiece, and that's *Goto: Island of Love*. That can rank alongside the great films in the history of cinema. I'd put *Immoral Tales* in the masterpiece class too. The other Borowczyk films are often as fascinating, often more grotesque - certainly more sexually explicit - but probably not as wholly satisfying as *Goto: Island of Love* - from a conventional critical standpoint. But *The Beast, Blanche, Behind Convent Walls*, and *Love Rites* would count as extraordinary films by most standards.[2] They may not be quite up there with *Persona* (Ingmar Bergman) or *8 1/2* (Federico Fellini), but taken together they form a group of works that mark Borowczyk out as a maverick original. Similarly, Borowczyk isn't a filmmaker celebrated by critics or filmmakers, like Akira Kurosawa, Ingmar Bergman, Orson Welles, Federico Fellini, Jean Renoir or Sergei Eisenstein, and his films don't make critics' top ten lists.

You probably won't know many other people who've

2 For detractors, Borowczyk's films were better when they concerned ideas rather than the senses - philosophy not sex.

even heard of Walerian Borowczyk, let alone seen one of his films. His reputation as a producer of European arty porny films (art-as-porn films or porn-as-art films) is probably all that many people will have heard of him (movies with sex and nudity do seem to travel well). Needless to say, Borowczyk's films are *not* shown regularly on television (in Britain at least), even by channels which boast of their open-mindedness and international film broadcasts. I can think of maybe one occasion when *Goto: Island of Love* was shown in Britain in 25 years, but I may be wrong about that.

Similarly, you won't see Walerian Borowczyk's pictures at the cinema nowadays, even rep and arthouse and independent cinemas rarely screen his films. It's mainly home video releases (and, later, home DVD releases) that's enabled Borowczyk's films to reach a contemporary audience (the porny and arty elements make them perfect for niche marketing to the cognoscenti). And you'll have to hunt to find them all. You won't find *The Beast* next to *Back To the Future* and *Bad Boys* on the 'B' shelf in your local video store.[3]

Another problem with assessing Boro's work is the quality of the prints, DVDs and videos available – this is a fantastically visual filmmaker, but some prints are so washed out and nasty. Then there's the aspect of the sound and dubbing: some Borowczyk movies are only available in dubbed versions, rather than the much-preferred original sound plus subtitles.

3 Even the ten films available in the U.S.A. and Britain are difficult to track down – you'll have to try the usual places – amazon.com, ebay.com – but there'll be plenty more hunting around to find the rarer items.

As copies of some of Walerian Borowczyk's thirteen live action feature films aren't easily available, they won't be included in this book: *Bloodbath of Dr Jeckyll* and *Lulu*. I haven't seen *Blanche* and *La Marge* for a long time, so I have only included my notes on those films, written when I saw them. It's frustrating that so many of Borowczyk's 14 feature flicks (13 live action movies plus one animated film) are hard to find. Especially when there's so much other dreck readily available.[4]

However, for a time Walerian Borowczyk's films were popular, or at least they were on general release. According to David Cook's *A History of Narrative Film* (one of the best books on cinema *ever*, a total must-have), *The Story of Sin* was the most popular film in Poland in 1975, and *Immoral Tales* was the second most popular film in France in 1974 (that means a *lot* of people saw it – the French love movies more than almost anyone in the world).[5]

They *are* an acquired taste, but once you've seen a Walerian Borowczyk film, you don't forget it. No one else makes movies quite like Borowczyk's; the word 'unique' is thrown around a lot in critical circles, about this or that writer, this or that actor, this or that dancer. But Borowczyk's films truly are unique. As soon as that classical organ music starts up, completely distinctive, you know you're entering Borowczyk Land, a very strange place. Music's a big part of the Borowczyk world:

4 You can see some of Borowczyk's short films on the excellent UbuWeb Film site (ubu.com), and also YouTube (youtube.com).
5 C. Tohill, 55. Cinema admissions in 1973 were 176 million, down from 276 million in 1964.

you won't hear music like this anywhere else in cinema – and certainly not in *these* contexts. Again, many filmmakers are cited as having a distinctive way of using music – Martin Scorsese, Stanley Kubrick, Robert Altman – but Borowczyk's music has carved out its own niche. I must stop using the word 'unique' to describe Borowczyk's cinema, but he really is a man of unique talents.

You probably won't recognize many of the people in Walerian Borowczyk's films. He didn't use big stars, except once: Sylvia Kristel, darling of the Euro art film/porn scene in the mid-1970s. There are some recognizable actors in some of Borowczyk's films, though: Patrick Magee, Udo Keir, and Joe Dallesandro, but everyone else is a French, or Italian or German actor you've probably never seen before (or since).

Walerian Borowczyk's films are completely un-politically correct. But you probably already knew that. It's not that Borowczyk sets out to offend (although there is something of the trickster, the Surrealist *épater* of the bourgeoisie about Borowczyk, as with many artists). Rather, Borowczyk simply puts in his films what he wants.

⚜

Born on September 2, 1923 in Kwilcz in Poland, Walerian Borowczyk died on February 3, 2006, in Paris. Borowczyk studied at the Cracow Academy of Fine Arts (Andrzej Wajda was a fellow student), as a painter. Borowczyk wrote as well as directed most of his films; that's a very important point: it means that Borowczyk was much closer to being the true 'author' of his films than directors for hire (and even many celebrated directors *don't* also write their own movies). It also means that Borowczyk was largely the *originator* of his films: they didn't come from some outside influence or source, like a film producer or studio. (Other well-known Polish filmmakers include: Andrzej Wajda, Andrzej Munk, Jerzy Skolimowski, Krzystzof Zanussi, Roman Polanski and Krzysztof Kieslowski).

Based in Paris for much of his life (with his films made in French),[6] after moving there from Poland in 1958, Walerian Borowczyk was a painter and illustrator who went on to make short animated films (which included *Holy Smoke* (1963), *Le Jeux des Anges* (1964), and *Le Dictionnaire de Joachim* (1965)). Borowczyk's first animations were made with Jan Lenica (1928-2001)[7] – *Dom, Love Requited,* and *Once There Was.*

Other early films (some only a few seconds long) included *L'Ècole* (1958), *Dom* (1958), *Les Astronautes* (1959), *Le Concert de M. et Mme. Kabal* (1962), *Renaissance* (1963), *L'Encyclopédie de grand-maman* (1963), *Rosalie* (1966), *Diptique* (1967) and *Gavotte* (1967). In his animations, Walerian Borowczyk employed a variety of techniques, including pixillation, loops, collage, and painting on the film itself.

Les Astronautes was a wonderful comic adventure film (made with Chris Marker) about a man who constructs a bizarre spaceship and takes it into space, to the moon and beyond. There's visual and comic invention aplenty in *Les Astronautes*, and all manner of techniques are employed in the visual treatment, from

---

6 Most of Borowczyk's feature films were made in French, and in France. He also shot in Italy and Poland.
7 Lenica emigrated to Paris in 1963.

tinted black-and-white stills, to stop motion animation, captions, smoke effects, and live action. Walerian Borowczyk and Chris Marker mix up the animation techniques into a dazzling whole. And there's a typically Borowczykian moment when the man flies his rocket ship next to an apartment and spies on a half-naked woman in a window.

In *The School*, black-and-white still photographs depict a soldier being irritated by a fly, classic Surrealist Borowczyk humour. In *L'Encyclopédie de grand-maman*, Borowczyk indulges again in his love of early photographs. *House* (*Dom*) has moments of erotic intensity, which would become a staple of Borowczyk's cinema: a woman (played by Boro's wife, Ligia Branice), caresses and kisses the bust of a man. In *Renaissance*, a host of objects (such as an owl, a brass horn, a table and some books) are re-animated – putting themselves back together from a state of chaos and disrepair. *Scherzo Infernal* (1984) was a later work of animation, an outrageous, violent and comic satire on religion featuring grotesque demons.

Walerian Borowczyk's short films have a beauty, a mystery, a texture which's absolutely compelling. And the brilliant use of sound – of sound effects and music – should also be mentioned (although the visuals are so hypnotizing, coming thick and fast, it's easy to forget how much of the impact of these short films comes from sound).

Walerian Borowczyk's first feature film was the singular *Goto: Island of Love* (1968), although a feature of his collected animation was released before that: *Le*

Théatre de M. et Mme. Kabal (1967). *Goto: Island of Love* was followed by *Le Phonographie* (1969), *Blanche* (1971), *Une Collection Particulière* (1973), *Contes Immoraux* (*Immoral Tales,* 1974) and *Histoire d'un Péché* (*Story of a Sin*, 1975).

La Bête (*The Beast,* 1975) was Walerian Borowczyk's most controversial film, a mixture of French farce, surrealism, and a lot of sex (including bestiality). Borowczyk's next film, *La Marge* (1976, *The Margin,* a.k.a. *The Streetwalker* and *Emmanuelle '77*) again combined eroticism and surrealism; it was based on Borowczyk's friend André Pieyre de Mandiargues' novel, and starred Sylvia Kristel (of the *Emmanuelle* films) and Joe Dallesandro (of Andy Warhol's coterie).

Other films followed, including *Briefe von Paris* (1975), *Interieur d'un Convent* (*Behind Convent Walls,* 1977), *Belt of Fire* (1978), about the mass murderer Gilles de Rais, *Les Héroïnes du Mal* (*Three Immoral Women,* 1979), *L'Armoire* (1979), *Collections Privées* (1979), *Lulu* (1980), taken from Frank Wedekind's two plays (which had formed the basis of *Pandora's Box*), *Bloodbath of Dr Jeckyll* (a.k.a. *Blood of Dr Jeckyll* and *The Experiment,* 1981), *Ars Amandi* (*The Art of Love*, 1983), based on Ovid, episodes of *Série Rose* (1986-1991), and 1988's *Cérémonie d'Amour* (a.k.a. *Love Rites*). *Love Rites* starred Mathieu Carrière as a man who meets a prostitute (Marina Pierro) on the Paris Métro. Pierro, who had starred in *The Art of Love,* was superb as the mysterious, eternal prostitute, a mythical figure recalling the 'holy whores' of ancient religions.

Many of these European art films contained

Walerian Borowczyk's trademarks – surrealism, sex, violence and bizarre incidents. In 1986, Borowczyk made *Emmanuelle 5*, which seemed to confirm his softcore porn status for detractors. In tackling the *Emmanuelle* franchise, though, Borowczyk sent it up (there was a scene set at the Cannes film festival, with audiences clamouring to see a fictional porn film, *Love Express*).

The era of the 1960s and 1970s was a time when films with graphic sexual content, including porn films, entered the mainstream, or at least were widely distributed, and became chic. It was the era of *Deep Throat, Ai No Corrida, Last Tango In Paris* and *I am Curious, Yellow* (1997's *Boogie Nights* is a marvellous visit to the Seventies porn boom). It was a time when relaxed censorship regulations, the new permissiveness, the sexual liberation, the Pill, audiences demanding more liberal films, and other factors, enabled filmmakers to depict more sex and nudity in their movies.

As well as porn manufacturers, 'serious' filmmakers began to include 'X' rated or 'adult' material. So you have Bernardo Bertolucci showing sodomy in *Last Tango In Paris*, Nagima Oshima depicting penetration in *In the Realm of the Senses*, Pier Paolo Pasolini including erections in his 'Trilogy of Life' films, and so on. Borowczyk's pictures were very much part of this culture – or at least, they were *received* and *interpreted* within this porn/ art, art film/ porn film context.

Among the regular collaborators in Walerian Borowczyk's movies were actors such as Marina Pierro and his wife Ligia Branice, DPs Guy Durban and Bernard Daillencourt, production designer Jacques D'Ovidio,

Dominique Duvergé (AD and production manager), and writer André Pieyre de Mandiargues.

Walerian Borowczyk's films, like so many European films which have a life outside their country of origin on the international market, have a bewildering number of alternative titles (only a tiny percentage of movies ever get shown outside their country of origin). *La Bête* is also known as *The Beast, The Beast in Heat* and *Death's Ecstasy. Cérémonie d'amour* (1988) was *Queen of the Night* in the U.S.A., and also *Rites of Love* or *Love Rites*. *Docteur Jekyll et les femmes* (1981) was titled *The Blood of Doctor Jeckyll, The Bloodbath of Doctor Jeckyll* (the British cut version), *Bloodlust, Dr. Jeckyll and His Women* (the American dubbed version), *Dr. Jeckyll and Miss Osbourne*, and *The Experiment* (the British censored version). *Les Héroïnes du mal* (1979) is variously *Heroines of Evil, Heroines of Pain, Immoral Women* and *Three Immoral Women. Behind Convent Walls* (*Interno di un convento*, 1977) is also *Sex Life in a Convent* and *Within a Cloister. La Marge* (1976) is also *The Margin, Emmanuelle '77* and *The Streetwalker.*

⚜

Walerian Borowczyk quickly gained a reputation for producing erotic and (what some people saw as) pornographic material, combined with beautiful, painterly image-making, in which objects and details were given as much weight as people ('I attach a great deal of importance to details', Borowczyk said [J. Gerber, 173]). I don't regard Borowczyk's films as 'pornographic' at all (my own views are resolutely anti-censorship and pro-erotic. If that also means pro-pornography, fine).

There *is* a lot of nudity in Walerian Borowczyk's flicks, compared to the regular Hollywood film, or mainstream flicks in Europe and Asia. But not so extreme when compared to the European art film, which does occasionally have plenty of nudity. Or porn, of course.

However, it can be historically justified in another respect: go into any major art museum around the world and you'll probably encounter hundreds of naked bodies. From the Renaissance onwards nudity has been a regular element in high art (and of course in the art of the ancient world). By the time of the 19th century, academy and classical nudes are everywhere. There's Perseus rescuing Andromeda from the serpent, and she's naked; there's Cleopatra or Aphrodite reclining in her boudoir, and she's naked; there's a bunch of nice young boys swimming in a river, and they're naked. And it's obvious that painters and their patrons were choosing mythological or historical subjects (as opposed to Christian or Biblical ones) precisely so they could depict naked men and women. You couldn't show the Virgin Mary naked, but you could show the Goddess Venus naked. There's no doubt that the fine art nude is a classy, upmarket form of lowbrow, populist tits and ass.

If you have a few million dollars to spare and fancied funding some film adaptions of classic erotic books – *Fanny Hill, Moll Flanders, The Romance of Lust, The Perfumed Garden,* and of course *The Kama Sutra* – Walerian Borowczyk is without question the filmmaker for the job, in the entire history of cinema.

At times it seems as if Walerian Borowczyk were the reincarnation of some mediæval French monk, or an eighteenth century dandy, or an aristocratic acquaintance of the Marquis de Sade, or some highly intellectual æsthete like J.-K. Huysmans' Des Esseintes, a nobleman with a penchant for European painting and high-class pornography.

✤

I've mentioned Walerian Borowczyk in relation to pornography a few times in this book, but the connection lies more in the minds of the people – critics, fans, viewers – watching and discussing Borowczyk's films, than in the films themselves. I don't think the naked human body is pornographic, or showing it is pornographic, and nearly all of so-called pornography is really erotica, designed as entertainment. Rather, the emphasis on extreme violence and suffering in, for instance, Hollywood movies, is way more 'pornographic' than Borowczyk's films. There's male rape, for example, in movies like *Pulp Fiction, The Shawshank Redemption* and *Deliverance,* and some dubious depictions of sadomasochistic acts in pictures like *Misery, Frenzy,* and *Suspiria.* But those films don't have the stigma of pornography attached to them. And the level of violence and gore in movies such as *Black Hawk Down, Sin City* and *300* is so repulsive, so extreme. There's a sickening emphasis on aggression and physical pain which I regard as psychotic. It's the kind of thing cultists and martyrs would get off on in the early Christian era – all those religious obsessives who whipped themselves or lived in holes in the ground.

✤

Information on Walerian Borowczyk is scant, to say

the least. I mean, way scanter than many other lesser-known filmmakers. You have to really hunt and dig around. Of sources that are readily available, I'd recommend David Cook's *A History of Narrative Film*. There's a useful chapter on Borowczyk in *Immoral Tales: Sex and Horror Cinema in Europe 1956-1984*, by Cathal Tohill and Pete Tombs, a really marvellous movie book. About the best introduction to Boro you'll find. J. Gerber's book on the film producer Anatole Dauman includes a section on Borowczyk. Michael Richardson has a chapter on Boro in his *Surrealism and Cinema* (details on these books are in the bibliography).

Walerian Borowczyk is often mentioned in guide-books to European and world cinema, but the entries are usually short and not particularly useful, merely repeating the same facts. Similarly, on the internet, there is information on Borowczyk, but not much, and so websites that I would recommend are few. Imdb.com is always good, and Senses of Cinema, and the Movie Review Query Engine (mrqe.com).[8] I have included a filmography of Borowczyk, because apart from places like the Internet Movie Database, it's difficult to find.

In short, Walerian Borowczyk deserves to be much better known in film circles, and his movies deserve to be seen (compared to the dreck which consumes 99.9% of the global media market). But Boro's films seem destined to be lumped with exploitation cinema, softcore porn, mondo cinema, and arthouse cinema, perpetually on the outer reaches of world cinema. (And Borowczyk's films

8 There's a terrific gallery of Borowczyk's art at Animation World Network: awm.com/ gallery/boro/info

are difficult to track down; only ten are currently available in Britain, and you'll need to search hard to find them).

WALERIAN BOROWCZYK, WOMEN AND PORNOGRAPHY

Walerian Borowczyk was a *connoisseur* of erotica, as his films bear out, and had a small museum of erotic objects. Like many an erotic addict, Borowczyk was in love with the female form and sex. His movies are full of images of naked or semi-nude women, like painterly studies out of the art of J.A.D. Ingres, Titian or Peter Paul Rubens, the camera often lingering on their pudenda and pubic hair, their breasts, or close-ups of their mouths. Often, Borowczyk's women are alone, engaging in autoerotic, narcissistic acts, like the women in high art: bathing, admiring themselves in a mirror, or, unlike in high art, caressing some object, and masturbating. Few filmmakers have as many images of masturbation, particularly female masturbation, in their works as Walerian Borowczyk.

Walerian Borowczyk favoured slim, young women in his films. At least in the lead roles. The fleshly, curvy figures of the art of Aristide Maillol or Eric Gill or Peter Rubens are much rarer in his cinema. He didn't go for the super-mammary women of Russ Meyer, either (and Borowczyk's camera lingers more over hips, asses and vulvas than breasts. But he clearly fetishized everything, and memorably mouths). If one were being socially conscious and right-on, one could also remark that Borowczyk favoured white women, not black or Asian women.

Walerian Borowczyk has never been simply a high-class eroticist, as his detractors have asserted (I don't regard him as a pornographer at all – but a lover of erotica, certainly). He shoots from a finished script, and pays special attention to the set, the design, and the many unusual props and objects in the frame. (It would take a long time to find and rent/ buy all the props and furniture for a Borowczyk movie).

But Walerian Borowczyk's cinema seems to have been over-shadowed by the nudity and porno elements, with viewers and critics seeing that and not much else. A pity, because there's so much more going on in Borowczyk's films than nude bodies and fucking. And there's also a feeling that Borowczyk wasted his talent on worthless films. So that his career begins strongly, with *Goto: Island of Love*, *Blanche* and *Immoral Tales*,[9] but deteriorates to the crass level of *Emmanuelle 5*. There's a view that Borowczyk would have done so much better if he'd concentrated on some really challenging subjects, something that was worthy of his talent.

That's one view. Fine. But the facts don't bear it out. For instance, *Love Rites*, released in 1988, is a great Walerian Borowczyk film – the equal, I'd say, with *The Story of Sin*. So it wasn't really a 'decline' into

9 *Contes Immoraux* continued Walerian Borowczyk's exploration of the erotic (for some it was a lapse into pornography, as Borowczyk's next film, *La Bête*, demonstrated for those nay-sayers).

mediocrity and dirty old man territory, because *Love Rites* shows Borowczyk enjoying himself immensely with a tale of man who gets involved with a prostitute in modern-day Paris and discovers more than he bargained for. *Love Rites* is not porn, not smut, not a dirty old man leching after acres of young naked flesh.

And since the late 1990s and early 2000s, there has been a liberalization in film censorship/ classification (in Britain), with a bunch of films reaching more mainstream markets which have been trumpeted for containing more sexually explicit material. Yes, you can see cocks and cunts at play in films like *Romance, Intimacy, Pola X, 9 Songs* and others, but those movies aren't a patch on even the lesser Borowczyk films.

Is Walerian Borowczyk's cinema sexist or misogynist? It's hardly worth even bothering to address the question, because most every feminist or critic who looks at Borowczyk's films will be certain of his out-and-out sexism and his blatant misogynism. A feminist would say 'is there a moment in Borowczyk's cinema when he *isn't* misogynist or sexist?' Borowczyk himself, though, clearly didn't hate women, or fear them, or whatever. But his films contain plenty of ammunition for evidence of fear, anxiety, neurosis and all the rest of it about women.

I don't like to say 'misogynism' in relation to Walerian Borowczyk: I don't think woman-hating is part of Borowczyk's cinema or philosophy at all. The opposite, in fact (but feminists counter that worshipping women can be as bad as disliking and fearing them).

What's striking, though, while we're on the subject of women and feminism, is just how many of Walerian

Borowczyk's films feature women in the lead roles. *Blanche, Three Immoral Women, Immoral Tales, The Beast, The Story of Sin, The Streetwalker, Lulu, Emmanuelle 5, Behind Convent Walls, The Art of Love, Love Rites* – actually, it's *all* of Borowczyk's live-action films, apart from *Goto: Island of Love* and *Dr Jeckyll.* And that makes Borowczyk *very* unusual for a male film director, and for any major filmmaker.

For all its apparent sexism and misogynism, Walerian Borowczyk's cinema also contains some strong roles for women. Miriam in *Love Rites*, for instance, may be a sadistic prostitute, but she's also a strong, independent woman. And at the end of *La Bête* it's the two beasts that die, while the heroines survive (though damaged).

I wouldn't say that the sexism was any worse in Walerian Borowczyk's films than, say, the films of Jean-Luc Godard or Rainer Maria Fassbinder or many European art filmmakers (have a look at Godard's *Contempt* or *Prénom: Carmen*, for instance). But the sexism certainly is more overt, more obvious. Borowczyk's cinema reveals the sexism, the patriarchal laws, the social hierarchies in which women are secondary participants, much more vividly than many other European movies of the same era.[10]

Having considered Walerian Borowczyk's films for some time, I wonder if one of the reasons that some

10 Not to be under-estimated is Walerian Borowczyk's grasp of social conventions and hierarchies, which appear again in *The Beast*, and in many of his other movies: many of his cinematic worlds have clearly delineated social codes and relationships: everyone knows their place, everyone has their own situation and duties. Borowczyk is brilliant on social ritual and deference, on the manifestation of power relations within social groups. That he came from Eastern Europe only enhances his vision.

viewers find the concentration on sex and nudity off-putting is the way that Borowczyk incorporates it. Sex scenes and nudity are regular elements in movies – at least in the Western tradition, and have been since cinema was invented. But in Borowczyk's films, the camera lingers over parts of the body far, far longer than most movies do. And Borowczyk employs not one shot of a butt or a mound, but many. Hold on anything like that for too long and some viewers get uncomfortable. It's not that they don't wanna see nude bodies, whether male, female or whatever, it's that Borowczyk's films put viewers into a particular viewing position which makes their voyeurism palpable.

⚜

Walerian Borowczyk cast beautiful women in his leading roles: Sylvia Kristel, Ligia Branice, and Marina Pierro. If you were cast in a Walerian Borowczyk film, you'd be expected to strip off – completely (no body suits, no special clothes to hide bits you don't wanna show). You'd probably have to do a sex scene, and also some homosexual sex. You might have to run through fields or woods naked (and barefoot). But Boro and his casting assistants certainly had a knack for discovering terrific unknown actors (and performers willing to do a lot of crazy stuff).

There's more humour than one might think in Walerian Borowczyk's films. Not understanding the humour is part of the problem with viewing films with subtitles or dubbing (to test this – watch a movie in a language you don't understand with an audience that does understand it. You'll see a difference between the subtitles you don't think are particularly funny and the audience laughing).

But true eroticism, Walerian Borowczyk said, doesn't like laughter or jokes. True eroticism was a serious business, he remarked. Borowczyk though couldn't resist adding humour to sexual situations. He called *The Beast* more a comedy than an erotic film.

A film director who has employed even more nudity than Walerian Borowczyk – in terms of sheer numbers – is Peter Greenaway. There are similarities between Borowczyk and Greenaway, but not in the use of nudity and sex. In Greenaway's cinema naked bodies are presented in a cool, even cold, scientific and medical fashion. They are arranged as out of historical paintings but they look like people queuing up to be medically examined. Borowczyk's approach is much more openly erotic. He loves naked bodies (and not only women's). In Greenaway's cinema there a feeling of the filmmaker being ashamed or restrained even as he's fascinated by nudity. He wants to be a *European* filmmaker but can't quite shake off the repressed *British* side. In Borowczyk's cinema, he doesn't care about repression and such things, and is happy to linger at length over nude bodies.

MAKING A BOROWCZYK MOVIE

What was it like making a Walerian Borowczyk film? Here are some guesses. I don't know for sure, but I bet the hours were long on a Borowczyk shoot; I bet Borowczyk would carry on filming until he got what he wanted. I bet the actors had to rough it along with the crew (no comfy trailers, no comfy limos ferrying actors from comfy hotels miles away). I bet Borowczyk wouldn't have any time for actors who didn't want to do what they'd agreed to do (like stripping off or simulating sex).

I bet Walerian Borowczyk was meticulous to the point of driving everyone else in the crew nuts (I can imagine Borowczyk art directing scenes to the point of maddening detail – adjusting the way the folds in a dress lay on a bed, for instance, or having a painting hang on a wall in *just the right way*. The actress Grazyna Dlugolecka commented that Borowczyk moved actors around like puppets, and seemed to be more concerned with how props looked). I bet Borowczyk inspired a kind of grudging respect in his cast and crew.

It seems that Walerian Borowczyk shot everything, too, and didn't hand over shooting to second unit directors or assistants. In other words, you can sense Borowczyk's presence behind every scene. Sex film producer Alain Siritsky said that Borowczyk 'can do everything: write, lighting, set design, edit and even do the poster'.[11]

I imagine that producers and crew, as with Orson Welles or Alfred Hitchcock, wouldn't interfere with

11 Quoted in C. Tohill, 227.

Walerian Borowczyk's vision once the film had been agreed upon and was shooting. Borowczyk knew what he was doing and I bet producers and crew found it easier just to let him get on with it (film directors are well-known for not wanting to hear the word 'no' when they're shooting. All they want to hear is, 'yes, I think we can do that').

I doubt there were extensive rehearsal periods for the actors, or any rehearsal at all. Many Walerian Borowczyk scenes look as if the director has told an actor, 'OK, run along that path', 'How far?', 'I'll tell you when to stop'. And off they go.

And a lot of Walerian Borowczyk's scenes look as if the scene was just one take, and Borowczyk would say fine, print, let's go to the next set-up, put the camera over here by the Renoir nude, Julio. I doubt that Borowczyk asked for endless takes like Stanley Kubrick – partly because these were low budget films, and precious film stock would need to be used carefully. On the other hand, being a perfectionist would mean Borowczyk would likely keep going until it was close to being right.

BOROWCZYK IN THE INTERNATIONAL MOVIE MARKET

Remember, too, that Walerian Borowczyk's films were low budget affairs. By low budget, I mean truly *low budget*. They were shot on 35mm film stock, true (and thankfully), but Borowczyk would have been using budgets in the region of, I reckon, $200,000-400,000, and maybe even less. For comparison, Hollywood calls a film 'low budget' these days if it comes in at less than 30 million bucks. (When deciding what to spend the budget on, you can bet that Borowczyk made sure the costumes on each film looked right. And they did).

It was the same with Walerian Borowczyk's contemporaries, like Pier Paolo Pasolini or Jean-Luc Godard: their financers and distributors knew that there was an audience for the films of these *auteurs* within their country of origin. And if the subject matter was appealing (and nudity helped plenty), the films might be able to travel outside of their country of origin. One must never forget that only a *tiny fraction* of films made in Europe get released in cinemas outside their country of origin – in the 1960s and 1970s as now. You may think 1,000s of foreign language movies are widely available, but there are many thousands more that don't go beyond national borders. In other words, to get financed, the films must have been able to be sustained by the audiences of their own country (in other words, Borowczyk's films were low budget partly because they would only be seen predominantly in France or Italy).

Remember, too, that this was an era when ancillary markets were much smaller than today: no video, no DVD, no cable and satellite channels. Secondary markets of the 1960s-1970s would include television, and not much else. Only with the rise of home entertainment delivery systems in the Eighties would Walerian Borowczyk's films be able to generate revenue from areas outside of theatrical exhibition or television (and I bet quite a few of Borowczyk's films were rarely if ever shown on network TV).

But if we're talking about Walerian Borowczyk at all now, it means that his movies have had some life outside of their country of origin and their particular era. They have lived on, somehow. In itself, that's an amazing fact, because thousands of films and filmmakers have disappeared – from France, Italy, Spain, Germany, wherever in Europe, and will be remembered only by a few devotees.

In all, Walerian Borowczyk made 14 feature films, and originated the ideas for many of them. Only later did Borowczyk become a director for hire, with producers coming to him with offers. It changes things considerably when you're developing projects yourself – you have much more of yourself invested in them, for a start (but they often take much longer to get going and complete).

Only 14 films (and you'll be doing well to see them all, too). We might lament that Stanley Kubrick or Andrei Tarkovsky didn't make many pictures. But not Walerian Borowczyk, because he was making art before and after his feature film career. (One wonders, though, what Borowczyk might have done with a mega budget, with the vast resources of set construction, location shooting, extras and visual effects of a contemporary blockbuster movie. It would never happen, of course, for numerous reasons). If you want to take in the *Collected Works* of Ingmar Bergman or Jean-Luc Godard, though, you're talking about huge amounts of film, video, television, radio and theatrical work.

Another thing: thankfully, unlike some European art

films one could mention, Walerian Borowczyk's films are 90 to 100 minutes long. That's just right. No need for movies running two-and-a-half hours or more. No need for the misconceived length of *Céline and Julie Go Boating* or *The Damned* (*auteur* films which outlast their welcome).

WALERIAN BOROWCZYK AND GENRE

Walerian Borowczyk stuck to particular genres in his films, and didn't venture into, say, gangster flicks, or science fiction, or Westerns. Borowczyk is not interested in America at all, like so many of his European art film contemporaries, like Jean-Luc Godard, Wim Wenders or Rainer Werner Fassbinder. He doesn't quote from American movies, doesn't use American stars in his films, and isn't using American cinematic forms in his pictures. While filmmakers such as Godard were constantly critical of America yet talked about American cinema and recreated it in their films, Borowczyk just wasn't interested.

Walerian Borowczyk's movies remain resolutely *European*, the Old World not the New World, through and through (Werner Herzog and Ingmar Bergman resemble Borowczyk in this respect). There might have been overtures to Borowczyk from American film producers or studios, but Borowczyk preferred to remain in Europe to work. He didn't, like so many of his European contemporaries, 'go Hollywood' (and like so many European filmmakers right back to the early days of cinema). And while filmmakers like Jean-Luc Godard or François Truffaut remained in Europe but used American cinematic forms and ideas (and actors), Borowczyk never did. (However, he did work for some of the big names among European producers, such as Pierre Braunberger, Anatole Dauman, Alain Sarde, and the Hakim brothers).

And when we say that Walerian Borowczyk's movies are 'European', we also mean a very old idea of Europe. Borowczyk does deal with contemporary Europe, of course (not least with Communist Poland, his home country), and he does tackle the political and social situation in Europe from the 1950s onwards.[12] But, really, Borowczyk is interested in the idea of a Europe that stretches back into the 18th and 19th centuries, and into the Renaissance and the Middle Ages. And Borowczyk went right back to ancient Rome, with his play on the poet Ovid (Ovid was popular in the Middle Ages, in the courtly love tradition).

See, one of the most striking aspects of Walerian Borowczyk's cinema is that so many of his films were *historical*: they were costume dramas and history movies (and his first film – for some his best film – *Goto: Island of Love* – was one of the strangest historical pictures ever made). That's a long tradition in the European art film, of course: every European art filmmaker has delved into history. But only a few have made historical films as

12 Politics plays a huge part in Polish cinema, of course – and includes issues such as Communism, Solidarity, socialist realism, Marxism, liberalization, and continual confrontations and dialogues between the State and the film industry.

their basic genre or type of movie.

There's Werner Herzog, and Pier Paolo Pasolini. And if European art filmmakers go back into the past, it's usually into the 20th century, and in particular the middle years – leading up to and during World War Two. Borowczyk, though, loves to explore older cultures than that. And if he does do something set in the 20th century, it's the period *before* the First World War, before that war changed everything in Europe. (In this sense, Borowczyk's cinema is a perpetually *fin-de-siècle* cinema, always on the bring of collapse, always showing societies in decay).

⚜

It's important, too, to remember that Walerian Borowczyk was an artist and animator for a long time before moving into live-action features. In other words, he wasn't only a filmmaker through-and-through, and wasn't a filmmaker throughout his artistic career. By the time *Goto: Island of Love* was released, for instance, Walerian Borowczyk was 45. His feature film career is actually a period of around twenty years, from 1968 to 1988 – and after that he continued to make art, write short stories and have exhibitions. (He also directed some TV, including *Série Rose*, in 1988 and 1990.)

Walerian Borowczyk said that whatever the medium – film, short stories, painting – his creativity was the same. Jean-Luc Godard made similar remarks: film-making and writing were part of the same creative activity, and if he wasn't able to make movies, Godard said, he'd write. Borowczyk said he created very swiftly. 'I conceive all my films in an instant, and only objective means prevent me from making them in that instant' (D. Thomson, 2001).

⚜

I've mentioned how exotic and weird Walerian Borowczyk's films are, but there were many pictures made in the 1960s and 1970s which were just as crazy – I mean those movies labelled 'mondo cinema', or 'exploitation cinema', or 'sexploitation', or 'underground cinema'. And spoofing Catholic themes and imagery is a big part of those European movies (understandable, being as many were made in Italy, France and Spain). There are films about vampires, Dracula, Frankenstein, monsters, occultism, horror, Satanism, the Devil, nuns, and on and on, in 100s of films made in Europe from the 1960s to the 1980s, the era when Borowczyk was active in feature filmmaking.

And Walerian Borowczyk's flicks, with their eroticized nuns, their sex scenes and nudity, their sense of the grotesque, are very much part of low budget European filmmaking of the 1960s-70s, part of the cast of horror, sex, exploitation and *fantastique* films – the vampires, aliens, serial killers, babes and freaks. (And Hollywood and American TV of course recycles vampires and horror numerous times – the *Vampire Diaries, Underworld, True Blood* and the *Twilight* movie and TV franchises being recent examples).

Part of the reason is that horror, thriller and occult films are cheap to make. And that's also why so many of those movies include nudity – all you have to do is get people to take off their clothes. You don't have to build vast sets or have costly costumes. It's the same with porno films (and also why porn often takes up horror or sci-fi or occult genres). As low budget Spanish horror maestro José Larraz put it:

> When you have no money, the only guarantee for the box office is sex. How can I make a film like *The Spy Who Came In From the Cold* with inexperienced actors and no money?[13]

So although we exalt filmmakers such as Walerian Borowczyk or Pier Paolo Pasolini or whoever – because they are 'serious' filmmakers, filmmakers who've made some 'serious' work which can be properly called 'art' – there are hundreds of other filmmakers and films of that period which contain just as much outrageous imagery. I mean filmmakers like José Bénazéraf, Jess Franco, Jean Rollin, José Larraz, Massimo Pupillo, etc. Or maybe it's because, somehow, filmmakers like Pasolini, Robbe-Grillet and Borowczyk have survived, while so many others have been forgotten.

WALERIAN BOROWCZYK'S INFLUENCE

One can easily discern the influence of Walerian Borowczyk on filmmakers such as David Lynch, Terry Gilliam and Jeunet and Caro (the latters' films *Delicatessen* and *The City of Lost Children* contain references to Borowczyk's *Goto: Island of Love*. Indeed, *The City of Lost Children* is a virtual remake of *Goto* in

13 Quoted in C. Tohill, 199.

many respects, down to the humour, the surreal imagery, and the stylized, shabby wood and metal and stone *mise-en-scène*). Terry Gilliam said he and Terry Jones loved Borowczyk's *Goto: Island of Love* and *Blanche*. Of Borowczyk's short *Jeux des anges*, Gilliam said it was

> just extraordinary: the sense that you're on a train with the walls of the city going past, and then the sound of angels' wings – incredible... Terry Jones and I went crazy over Borowczyk because his films were so much about atmosphere and texture. (T. Gilliam, 39)

As well as Gilliam, the Quay Brothers and Neil Jordan have expressed their admiration for Walerian Borowczyk. (Jordan had a go at his own version of an erotic, Freudian update of a Grimm fairy tale in *Company of Wolves*, but although it's fêted in British film critical circles, *The Company of Wolves* ain't a patch on a Borowczyk movie).

Walerian Borowczyk has his fans among critics – such as Ado Kryou, David Thomson, Tom Milne, and Mark Kermode.

WALERIAN BOROWCZYK AND EROTICISM

Walerian Borowczyk's is a highly cultured cinema, a cinema of (for) connoisseurs – eclectic, subtle, mysterious and haunting. Many films were based on literary sources: Ovid (*Art of Love*), André Pieyre de Mandiargues (*The

Streetwalker and *Love Rites*), Robert Louis Stevenson (*Bloodbath of Dr Jeckyll*), Franz Wedekind (*Lulu*), and Stendhal (*Behind Convent Walls*). Borowczyk certainly delivered on one count: there was plenty of nudity, plenty of sex, but his films were also that rare thing, *erotic*.

André Pieyre de Mandiargues (1909-1991) is an important figure among Walerian Borowczyk's collaborators: he provided the stories for *La Marge, Love Rites,* part of *Immoral Tales,* and the narration, props and much of *Une collection particulière.* He also wrote the novel that was the basis for *Girl On a Motorcycle* (a.k.a. *Naked Under Leather,* Jack Cardiff, 1968). Aside from *Girl On a Motorcycle* and Borowczyk's films, no one else seems to have produced movies from de Mandiargues' fiction.[14]

⚜

Were there ever so many movies of one director so in love with women's torsos, bellies, hips, buttocks, thighs and vulvas? Walerian Borowczyk delights in the medium close-up of women's bodies, shot from the thighs to the belly. He has them turn this way and that, sometimes naked, sometimes draped with gauzy material, sometimes with the light shining from behind, sometimes in soft focus.

These shots go beyond softcore porn, or mere titillation, as detractors call them; they become painterly appreciations of form, shape, tone, colour. They recall

---

14 One of Borowczyk's short films, *Esgarot de Venus* (1975), was a document of the art of Mandiargues' wife, Bona Tibertelli De Pisis. It's a minor work in the Boro canon, partly because De Pisis's erotic art isn't very inspiring.

artists such as Eric Gill, Aristide Maillol and Auguste Rodin, sculptors who worshipped that part of the female form in bronze and marble. Walerian Borowczyk's endless images of women's bodies around the torso, buttocks and hips also recall 19th century nude paintings, by Gustave Moreau, Jean Auguste Dominique Ingres or Gustave Courbet, or the thousands of academy nudes.

Walerian Borowczyk certainly knows his history of religion and sex, the links between spirit and flesh, the Passion and pornography, extreme religious faith and erotic fervour, mysticism and masturbation. Among the 20th century artists who've addressed the fusion between sex and spirit are Georges Bataille, D.H. Lawrence, James Joyce, John Cowper Powys, Eric Gill, and directors such as Luis Buñuel, Ingmar Bergman and Pier Paolo Pasolini.

Walerian Borowczyk is certainly very much in the same tradition of *avant garde* and modernist European literature that explores sexual and religious issues in extreme manifestations: Borowczyk is part of the tradition which includes Surrealists like Hans Bellmer with his dolls and fingers penetrating orifices; or Georges Bataille with his pornography of asses, eyes, eggs and mouths in *The Story of O*; or the dreamscapes of arch Surrealist prankster Salvador Dali; or the far superior Surrealism of Luis Buñuel; or the man behind it all in France: the Marquis de Sade. And those writers who were just as extreme, and still part of that 'no limits' modernist tradition: Henry Miller, Pauline Réage, Jean de Berg, Emmanuelle Arsan, William Burroughs, D.H. Lawrence, Anaïs Nin, etc.

Walerian Borowczyk maintained that he wasn't a maker of erotic films, and disliked that kind of categorization. It was too narrow, for a start, and was more to do with how people perceived him and his films, than who he really was, or what his movies really were. Besides, Borowczyk said, sex was no more unusual than eating or smoking cigarettes. When an interviewer called him a pervert, he replied 'who isn't a pervert?'

When you look closer, you can see that Walerian Borowczyk's films aren't particularly pervy – especially when compared to many strands of pornography. Even Borowczyk's most controversial production, *The Beast*, depicts heterosexual sex (apart from the curé and his choirboys, which's not really shown). And everything the beast does with Romilda is within the bounds of regular heterosexual sex. Indeed, there are sexual depictions in mainstream films which are much more 'perverse' than the sex in *The Beast*. And pictures such as *Ai No Corrida* are way more perverse and objectionable, if you want to see them like that, than the sex in *The Beast* (in *In the Realm of the Senses* the lovers literally fuck themselves to death!).

Walerian Borowczyk defended his films by saying: 'all I do is express everyone's dreams'. It was odd, wasn't it, he maintained, that critics always talked about him, rather than the thousands of viewers and consumers who watched his movies. Borowczyk resisted that biographical approach of most film criticism, which always relates films to the filmmakers, which always says that *Citizen Kane* is always ultimately about Orson Welles (even more than about about William Randolph Hearst).

SOME OF WALERIAN BOROWCZYK'S INFLUENCES

Walerian Borowczyk lived in Paris for much of his life; Paris seemed to be a favourite destination for Eastern European and Polish filmmakers – Roman Polanski and Krzysztof Kieslowski ended up there (some directors, like Andrej Wadja, remained in Poland). And many other filmmakers gravitated towards Paris and France: Luis Buñuel, Raul Ruiz and Pedro Almodóvar. Why Paris? One reason is that France has one of strongest film cultures in the world: France produces more films than any country in Europe, and people go to the cinema more times a year in France than anywhere else in Europe. In short, it's a very good place to make movies.[15]

Aspects of French art in particular have long been interested (even obsessed) with sexuality and (Catholic) religion: Gustave Moreau, Félicien Rops, J.-K. Huysmans, Gustave Flaubert, Odilon Redon, Jean Delville, and the whole *fin-de-siècle* Symbolist and Decadent æsthetic movements. (Consider Rops' riotous, blasphemous images of Satan, devils, phalluses and naked women).

Walerian Borowczyk's sensuous, intellectual art cinema is clearly informed by the history of high European culture that goes back through the modernist *avant garde* and Surrealism, via Symbolism and *fin-de-siècle* Decadence, to the Romantics, to the Marquis de Sade and 18th century pornography, and further back, via Renaissance painting, to the flamboyance and

15 And most of Boro's movies were made in French, his second language. And with mainly French crews.

debauchery of the Medicis, the Borgias and Catherine the Great. Thence to mediæval religion and art (monasteries and convents, and the highpoint of Catholic art), bypassing the Dark Ages, to ancient Greek and Roman times.

One could analyze Walerian Borowczyk's cinema in relation to any of those eras and cultural movements. The affinities between Borowczyk's films and the Symbolist and Decadent age are obvious. For instance, *fin-de-siècle* 'high' culture was marked by 'gory exoticism', as Mario Praz put it in *The Romantic Agony* (289), by mysticism and black magic, occultism, Satanism, Catholic imagery, the macabre, the æstheticism of 'beauty', a love of costumes, dressing up, cross-dressing and dandyism, a love of Oriental and Byzantine culture, opulence and indulgence, where the key phrase is from Paul Verlaine: 'Je suis l'Empire à la fin de la décadence', Verlaine wrote in 1885 in 'Langueur' (1974, 180).

The age was summed up by works of literature such as Arthur Rimbaud's *Une Saison en Enfer*, Comte de Lautréamont's *Chansons de Maldoror*, Edgar Allen Poe's horror stories, Charles Baudelaire's *Flowers of Evil*, Gustave Flaubert's *Salambô* and *La Tentation de saint Antoine*, J.-K. Huysmans' *À Rebours* and *Là-bas*, Bram Stoker's *Dracula*, Joséphin Péladan's *Le Vice suprême*, and music such as Richard Wagner's *Parsifal*. (Some of the key artists of the Decadent and Symbolist epoch, apart from the writers and painters noted above, included Honoré de Balzac, Jean Moréas, Albert Aurier, Octave Mirabeau, Walter Pater, Jan Troop, Oscar Wilde, Pierre

Louÿs, Arnold Böcklin, Puvis de Chavannes and Stéphane Mallarmé.) Borowczyk is wholly at home in this cultural *milieu*, and draws on it.

Walerian Borowczyk is a follower of Surrealism, too – and Surrealism's preoccupation with sex and death, and with cruelty and absurdity, are an important element in his cinema. 'Beauty will be convulsive, or not all,' remarked the godfather of Surrealism, André Breton, and that's Borowczyk's maxim too.

Walerian Borowczyk also has the Surrealists' love of bizarre objects, and his cinema is full of them – from the fly-catching box in *Goto: Island of Love* to the metal finger extensions in *Love Rites.* (The fly-catching box, with its funnels ending in dog's hair, is a classic Surrealist device – it could be part of an exhibition by Max Ernst or Marcel Duchamp). And Borowczyk also employs Surrealism's use of juxtaposition: put two apparently innocuous objects together to form a third, strange being.[16]

Walerian Borowczyk's also fond of secret objects, objects that are hidden and have to be revealed – taken out of cabinets, or unfolded. In *La Bête* there's a family album with pages that are unfolded to reveal erotic drawings, and when a framed text is reversed it reveals a sketch of a horse coupling with a woman.

No need to mention the emphasis in Surrealism on dreams, on dream imagery, on the unconscious, or to cite Sigmund Freud or C.G. Jung *et al.* Walerian Borowczyk called *Immoral Tales* 'a sanctuary for liberty, an island

16 Of painters, Borowczyk said he was impressed by Tomasso Capelli, a 14th century Italian painter, Henri Lecourbe, and his own father (J. Gerber, 171).

of no restrictions': he has the 'no limits' philosophy of the Surrealists and the *avant garde* in Europe of the 20th century. 'All I do is express everyone's dreams', Borowczyk insisted: he was simply filming what every-body was dreaming about.

Carl Jung wrote:

> The cinema, like the detective story, makes it possible to experience without danger all the excitement, passion and desirousness which must be suppressed in a humanitarian ordering of society.

Linked to Surrealism is the Existentialism in Walerian Borowczyk's cinema: he is definitely a figure of the mid-to-late 20th century (or his artistic and political views seem to have been formed partly by the debates in Existentialism of the mid-century). There are also correspondences between Borowczyk's cinema and the Theatre of the Absurd of Samuel Beckett, Antonin Artaud and Eugène Ionesco. Part of that Existential belief is expressed in the cruelty and absurdity of modern life in Borowczyk's cinema. It's a view that encompasses pessimism, irony, and detachment. A view that sees the horrors of modern life and decides that not a lot can assuage them.

One of Walerian Borowczyk's notions was that Disney's films were more pornographic than his own (one imagines what the studio executives at the Walt Disney Company, viewing a DVD of *The Beast* or *Immoral Tales* beside their own *Aladdin* or *Bambi*, would make of that idea). Borowczyk said that *Snow White and the Seven Dwarfs* was much more erotic than any of his own films because of its 'stench of unsatisfied desire'.

Asked who'd he like to be in history if he had the choice, Walerian Borowczyk said: 'if I have to choose an epoch and an identity, it would be that of Leda's swan in antiquity (if she really was as beautiful as the artists represent her)' (J. Gerber, 172-3). The greatest representation of Leda is of course Leonardo da Vinci's lost painting – a copy gives some idea of the beauty of Leda.[17] There's also a lost version by Michelangelo Buonaroti, which's even more explicit: the giant swan lies between the woman's legs, its wing covering her vulva.[18] Both are known from copies.[19]

That is typical of Walerian Borowczyk's eccentricity – to be the swan that makes love to Leda. But the swan was of course a god – Jupiter – in disguise.

Bestiality is a recurring motif in Walerian Borowczyk's cinema. It crops up in *Three Immoral Women* (masturbation with a rabbit), in *The Art of Love*, where a character dreams of the mythical story of Jupiter tupping Pasiphæ, Queen of Crete in the form of a bull (characters also caress horse's genitals in *Ars Amandi*). The myth of Leda and the swan is of course one of the forerunners of Boro's penchant for human-animal interaction (and also *The Golden Ass* and *Beauty and the Beast*). *The Beast* is thus Boro's version of *Leda and the Swan*.

17 Leonardo's *Leda* was burned by Madame de Maintenon around 1700, or was destroyed by one of Louis XIII's henchmen.
18 There's a copy of *Leda and the Swan*, 16th century, in London's Royal Academy.
19 Anonymous, the 'ex-Spiridon version', *Leda and the Swan*, wood, 132 x 78cm, Rome; anonymous: *Leda and the Swan*, 112 x 86cm, Galleria Borghese, Rome.

WALERIAN BOROWCZYK'S VISUALS

Walerian Borowczyk has no superior when it comes to art direction in cinema. I reckon his art direction is the equal of celebrated examples, such as Cedric Gibbons and the MGM unit, or Walter Roehrig, Walter Reimann and Hermann Warm, who did the settings for *The Cabinet of Dr Caligari*. Is Borowczyk that good? Yes, I think he is.

Walerian Borowczyk has the credits of editor and production designer on many of his films. Many of the props and designs in Borowczyk's cinema have an appealing handmade feel to them, and I wonder if Borowczyk himself created some of them. You could mount an exhibition of the props in Borowczyk's films and it would be a great show (and more interesting than some other film exhibitions). A filmmaker such as Jan Svankmajer has a similar handmade, earthy feel to his props. In Borowczyk's cinema, it's the classic eroticization of the object – the (art) object as fetish.

One of Walerian Borowczyk's delights are boxes, cabinets, cupboards and display cases of all kinds – but preferrably nice old wooden ones. The cabinets and boxes often contain mysterious objects, like busts (Borowczyk is fond of statuary of all kinds). The sets of a Borowczyk film are *already* a museum display. They are like a Surrealist exhibition, or a 'secret museum' or 'private collection' of pornography and erotica of the 18th or 19th centuries. Or like a show of curios and antiques, arranged in old wooden display cases (recalling the Pitt Rivers Museum in Oxford, England, used so evocatively in Philip Pullman's *His Dark Materials* books).

Who knows where Walerian Borowczyk sourced all of the incredible objects in his films? Clearly some of them are manufactured just for the film, but many are existing pieces – partly because Borowczyk loves objects with a history, objects that have been used. Almost all of the objects in Borowczyk's pictures have been used; new, pristine objects are very rare in his films. So he must've scoured so many flea markets, antique stores, and art fairs.

The love of wooden boxes recalls all sorts of artists: the Surrealists loved boxes (like Max Ernst), as did the Minimal artists (like Donald Judd, Carl Andre and Jackie Winsor. Judd, one of the two or three most important artists of the 1960-2000 period, made the box his fundamental form). But there's one artist to consider in relation to the boxes in Borowczyk's cinema, and that the reclusive American artist Joseph Cornell, not least because of the way that Cornell would use his boxes to frame and present an arcane array of objects: a bird, a star map, an egg, a photograph, a feather, a pebble. If you like Borowczyk's films, I'd highly recommend you look at Joseph Cornell's enigmatic art of boxes.

Aside from *Goto: Island of Love*, Walerian Borowczyk's feature films were made in colour. Some of Borowczyk's animations were in black-and-white. It makes sense that *Goto: Island of Love* should be in black-and-white, but Borowczyk was clearly happy in either medium. (All of the usual constraints of commercial cinema would have operated for Borowczyk – all film producers, distributors and studios would argue for colour films, for all the usual reasons – one of the chief ones being – what else? – money). But if you consider the range of techniques that Borowczyk employed in his animation and films, you can see that he was a versatile and adaptable filmmaker. If a producer or studio told him he could only make films in colour or only in b/w or only with three actors or only with one set, he could do it, and flourish.

WALERIAN BOROWCZYK'S CLOTHES

Clothes, clothes, clothes, it's all about the clothes in a Walerian Borowczyk film. Even when there is plenty of other stuff going on, Borowczyk's films make time to study clothes. Many historical movies are called 'costume dramas', usually referring to the lovely frocks that the stars wear. But Borowczyk's films offer a real feeling for clothes – how they move on the body, how they hang on the body, and what is underneath them. Few other filmmakers have filmed clothes like Borowczyk: there is a heightened, sensual apprehension of the materiality of clothes, of textures, colours, shapes, etc.

Walerian Borowczyk could easily have had an alternative career as a fashion designer, or a costume designer for movies. (And Hugo in *Love Rites* is a fashion designer). Piet Bolscher, Borowczyk's regular costume designer (including the costumes in *Immoral Tales*), should be mentioned here (and the make-up and hair artists). *The Beast* is a costume drama. It's all about the clothes.

And no other filmmaker has so enjoyed characters putting on or taking off clothes. In *Immoral Tales* alone there are scenes of characters taking off their clothes in every episode, and sometimes it's a slow process, such as when Lucrezia's father and brother undress her. At times Borowczyk's films look like a costume fitting. And when characters take off their clothes in a Borowczyk picture, it's usually down to nudity.

Walerian Borowczyk of course loves layers and things that are hidden then revealed, or partially revealed. No one could fail to notice that this filmmaker has a fetish for naked women clad in gauzy, filmy cloth (usually white). Nipples and pubic hair are visible underneath; it's a classic look in erotica. To emphasize it, sometimes Borowczyk has actors take off their clothes then put on something see-through.

WALERIAN BOROWCZYK AND RELIGION

Walerian Borowczyk's films are anti-clerical and anti-Catholic; there are many scenes, in movies such as *Behind Convent Walls, La Bête* and *Story of Sin,* of the hypocrisy and sexual repression of Catholicism. At the same time, though, Borowczyk clearly revels in some of the imagery and ritual of Catholicism (like many filmmakers), and many of his films seem to ambiguously celebrate as well as condemn organized religion (one sees the same ambiguity in the films of Pier Paolo Pasolini,

Luis Buñuel and Federico Fellini).[20]

Like Pier Paolo Pasolini, Luis Buñuel and Ken Russell, Walerian Borowczyk delights in exploring the links between sex, death, religion, blasphemy and art. There is the same enjoyment in attacking institutions such as the church, Catholicism, morality and Christian tenets, using weapons such as Surrealism, sexuality, humorous irreverence, violence and blasphemy. Oh, and lots of nudity and sex.

Walerian Borowczyk was fascinated by institutions, and often portrayed them – the island of love in Goto, the convent in *Behind Convent Walls*, the Vatican in *Immoral Tales*, and the brothel in *The Rites of Lurve*. And he's also intrigued by dictatorships – Erzsébet Báthory presiding over her house of women in *Immoral Tales*, the Mother Superior in the nunnery in *Behind Convent Walls*, Goto on the island. And Borowczyk was especially adept at depicting the daily life of institutions, and the numerous rituals and daily tasks – the lighting of candles, say, or the preparation of a bathroom for a mistress, or the decoration of a church. There's a strong impression of the real daily lives of the people who live in these institutions. It's one of the strengths of *Goto: Island of Love*, for instance: you really believe those people are living in that degrading, shabby place. Borowczyk grounds his fantastical narratives in realism.

20 Walerian Borowczyk is a total one-off in cinema, but there are affinities between Borowczyk and filmmakers such as Pier Paolo Pasolini, Luis Buñuel, Werner Herzog and Jan Svankmajer (Pasolini, for instance, also liked to use unknown actors, shoot on location, explore Catholicism and religion, draw on the history of art, and use the ancient world).

ILLUSTRATIONS

Illustrations include:

✣ Some of Walerian Borowczyk's movies, including early short films. Plus artwork from home entertainment releases.

✣ Some references and correspondences with Borowczyk's cinema.

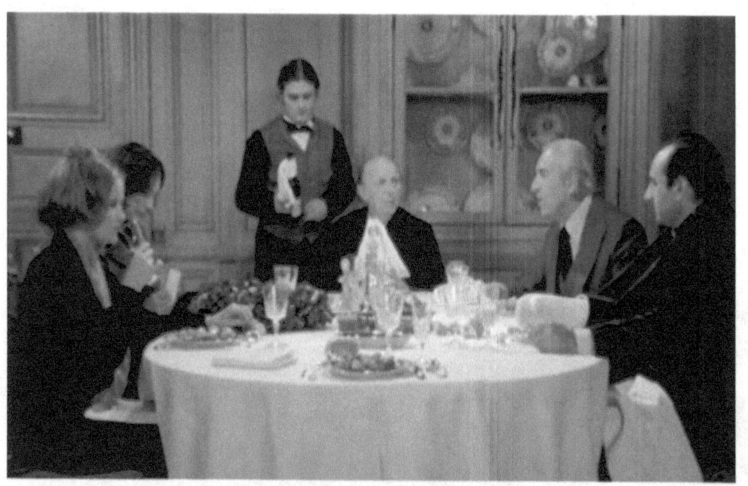

The key participants in the framing story in The Beast (above). And some kids that Clarisse 'borrows' from a friend (below).

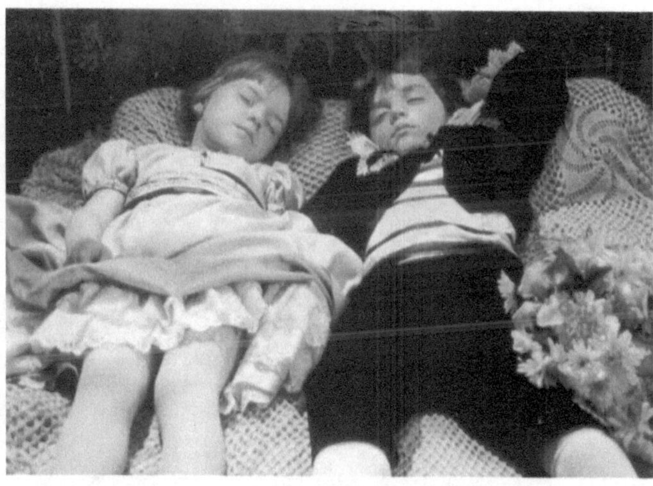

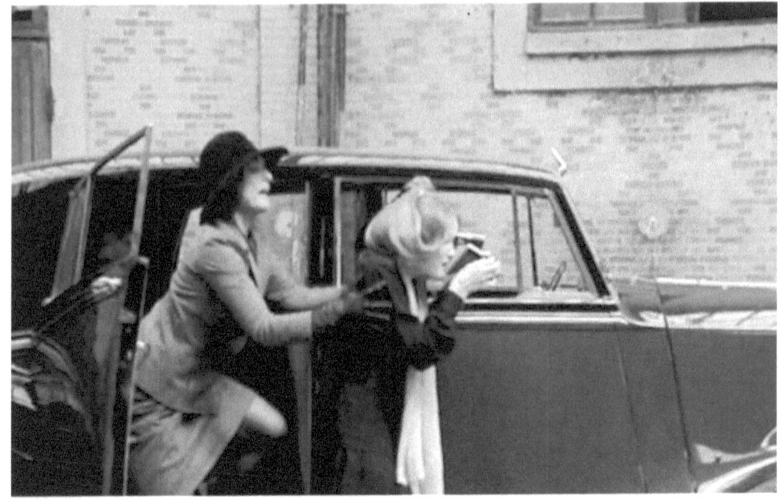

She arrives in a state of erotic excitement, as the curious princess of fairy tales. She ends the movie in a state of hysteria, naked, on the edge, thinking she's killed her beloved.

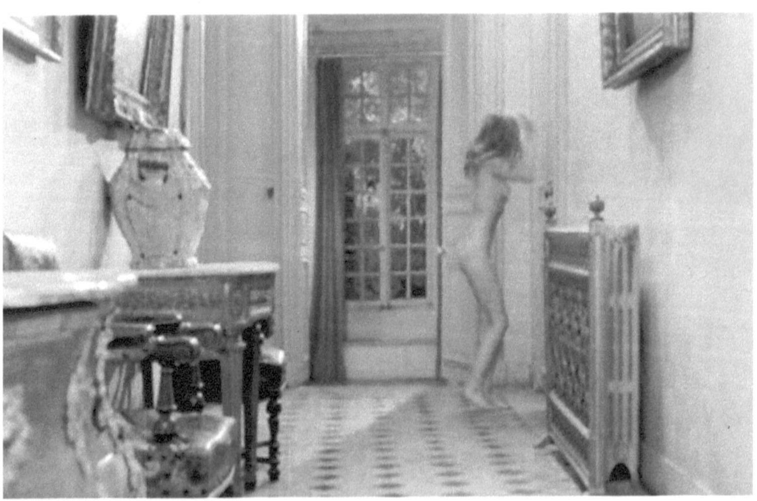

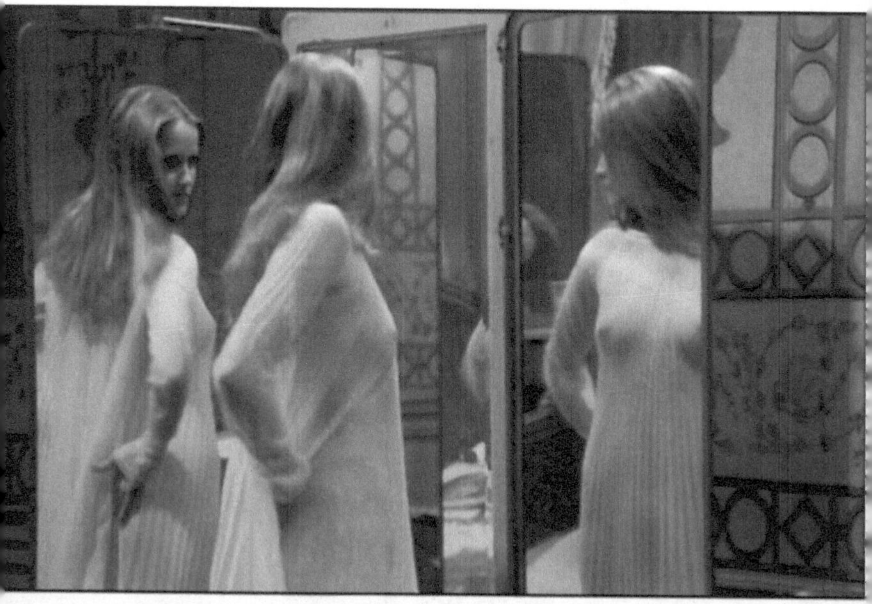

What filmmaker can resist mirrors?
Lucy in The Beast is another Borowczykian heroine who dresses in gauzy white and loses herself in autoerotic reveries.

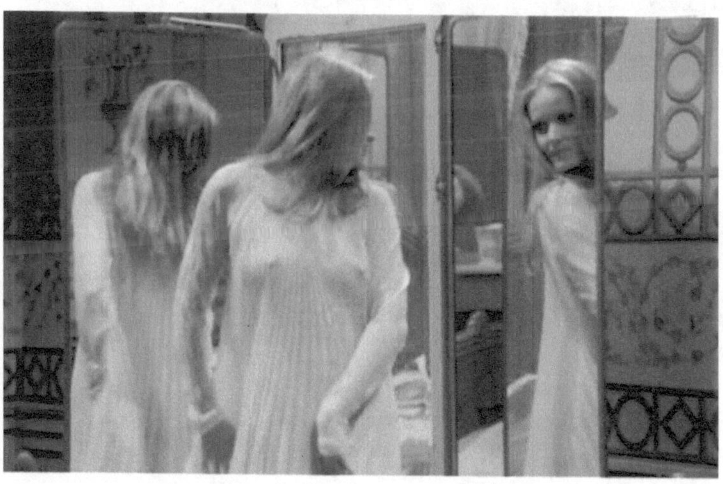

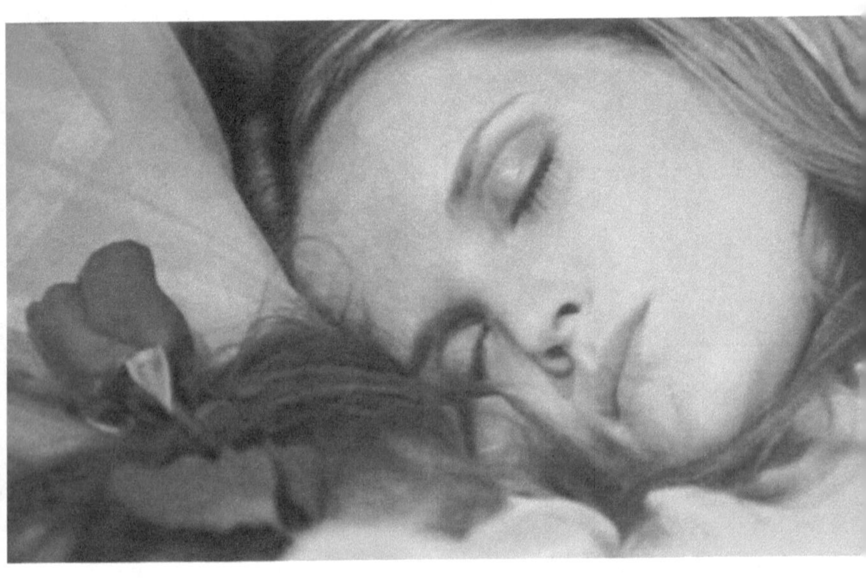

Belle dreaming of her beloved, beside the red rose he sent her.

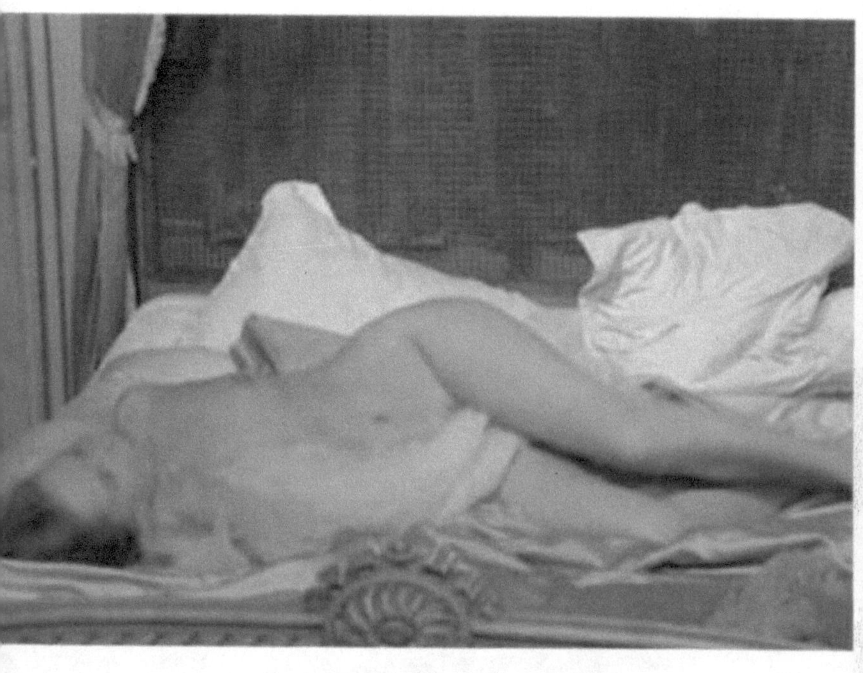

Women masturbating – a Walerian Borowczyk speciality.
Lucy in The Beast.

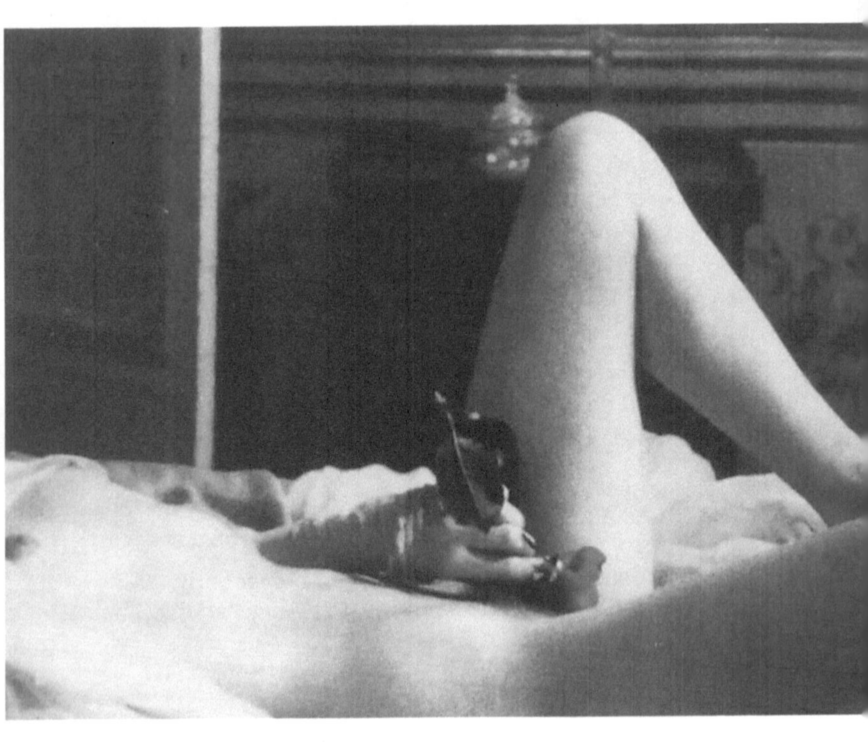

Masturbation and dreaming – Lucy using a red rose in The Beast as a sex toy, linking past and present.

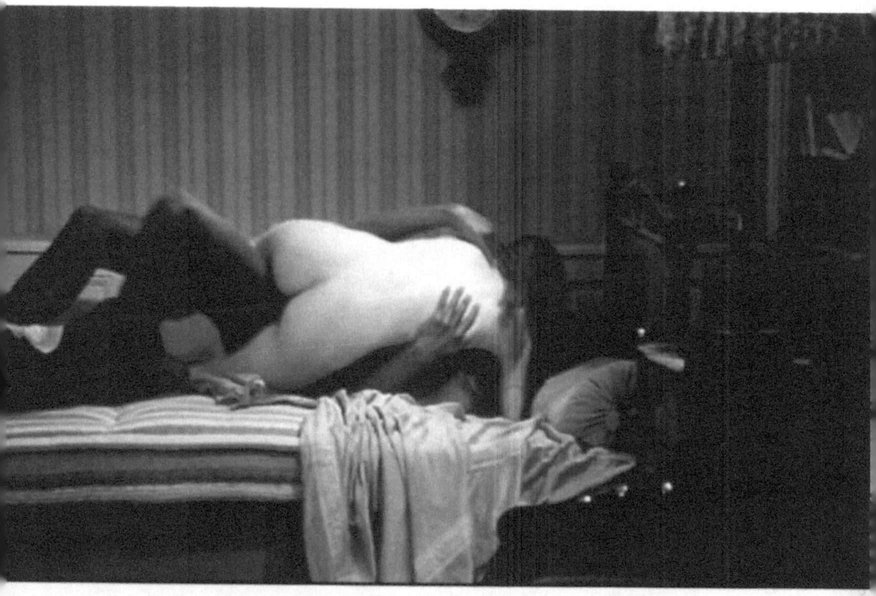

Everyone's perpetually aroused in The Beast:
Clarisse (Pascale Rivault) tupping Ifany (above).
And when he's called away, a headboard will do.

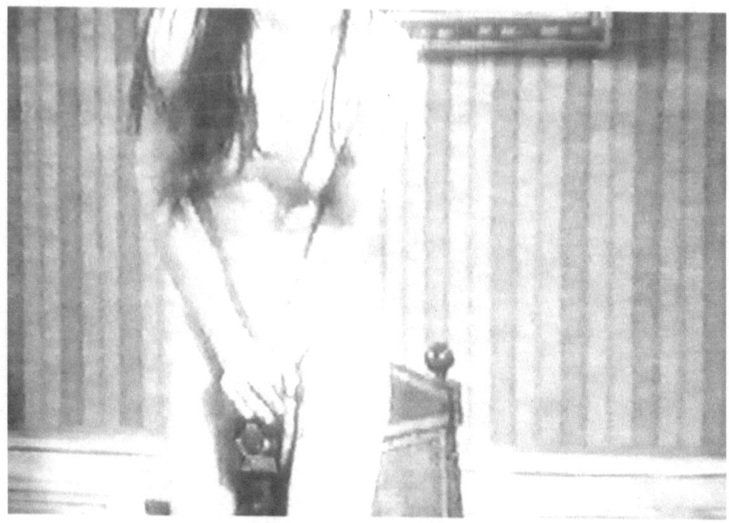

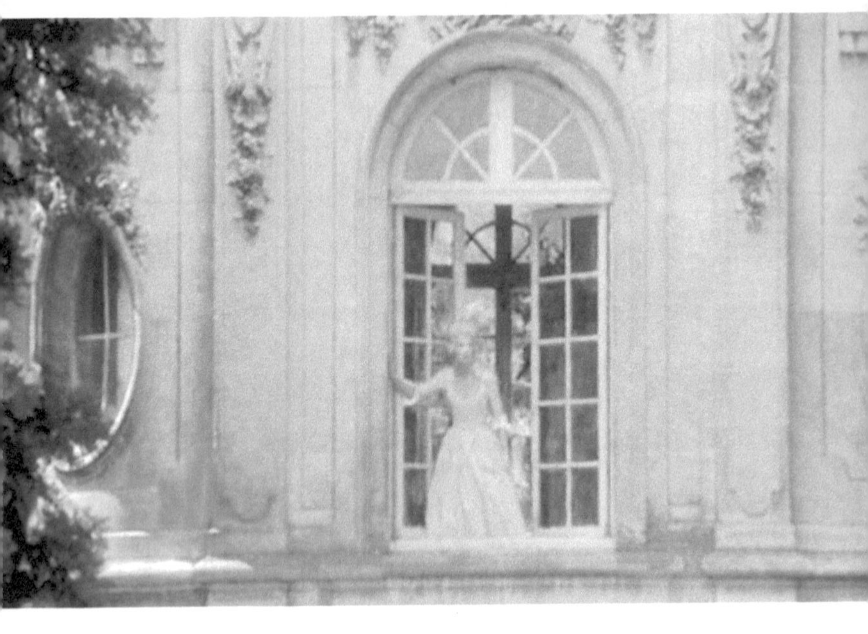

The legend starts out on a beautiful Summer's day, with Romilda playing the harpsichord in a pale blue dress.

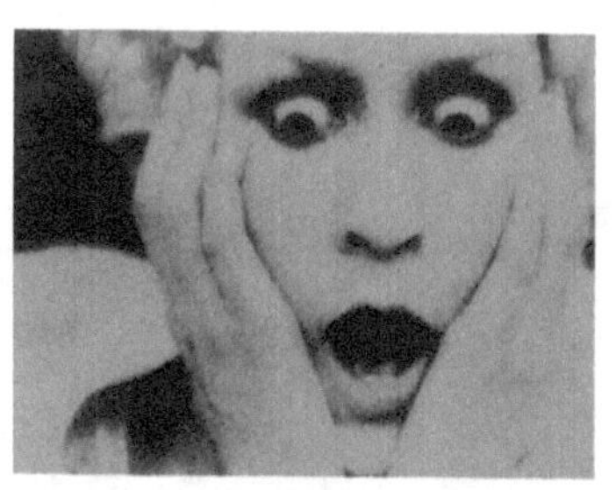

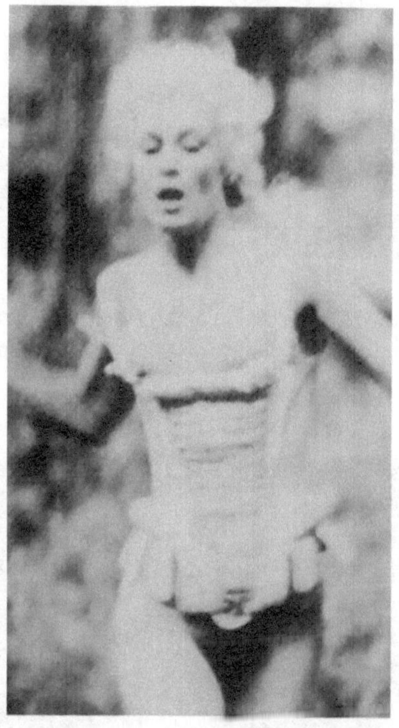

Sirpa Lane in Walerian Borowczyk's The Beast

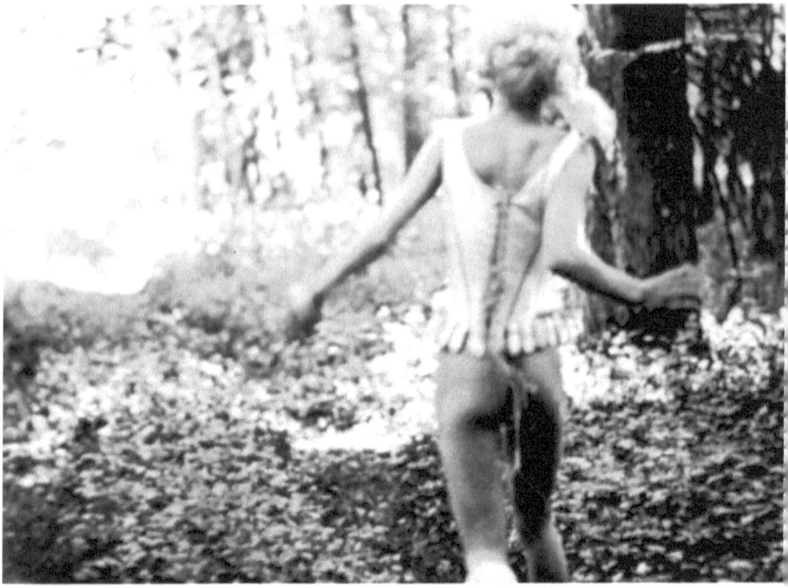

Walerian Borowczyk makes no apologies for bringing the subtext of a movie out into the open in The Beast

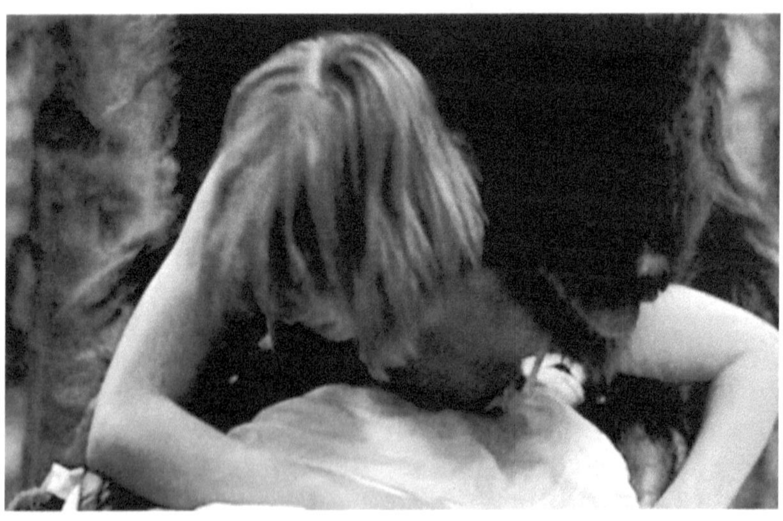

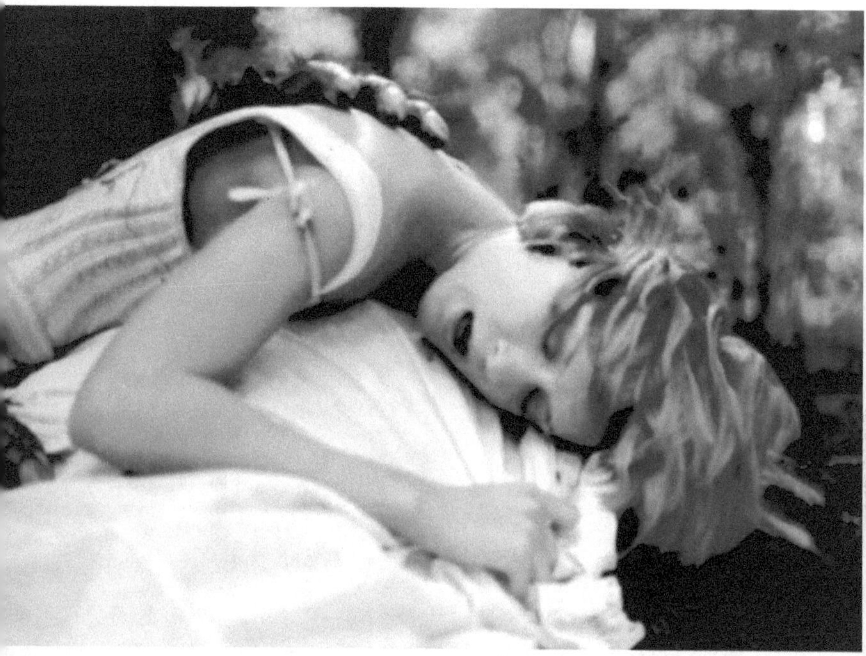

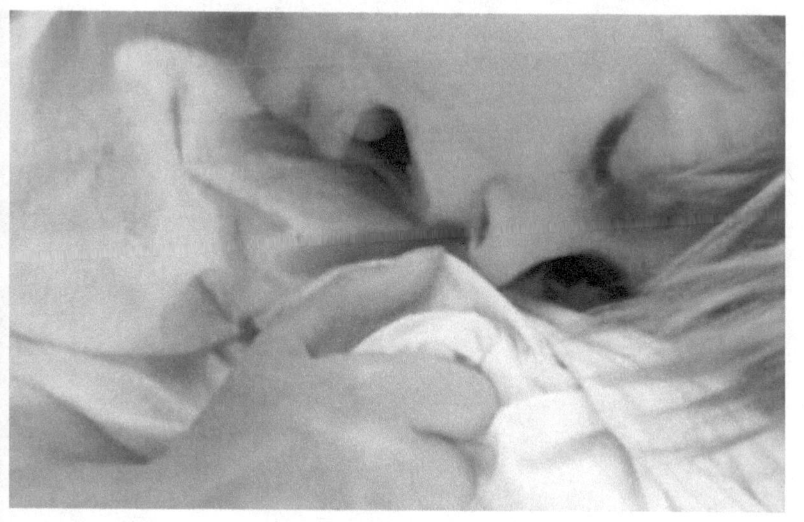

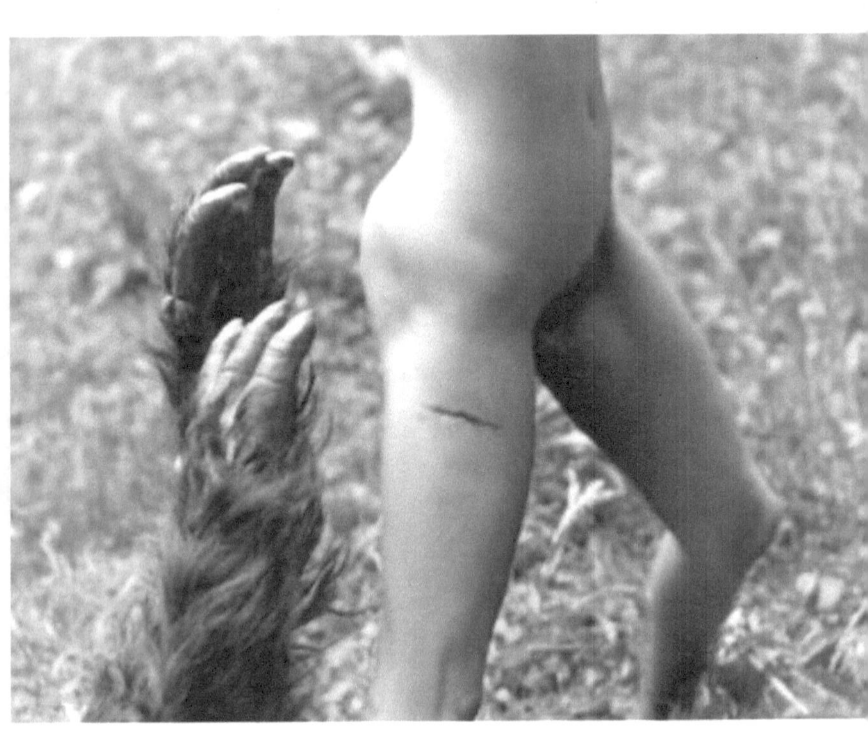

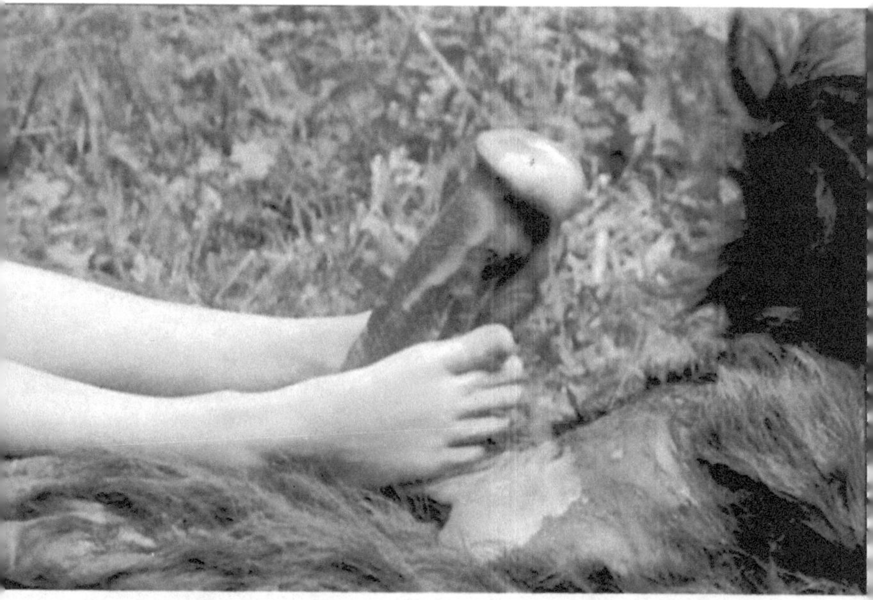

The filmmakers run thru the Kama Sutra and I Modi (The Ways) in The Beast

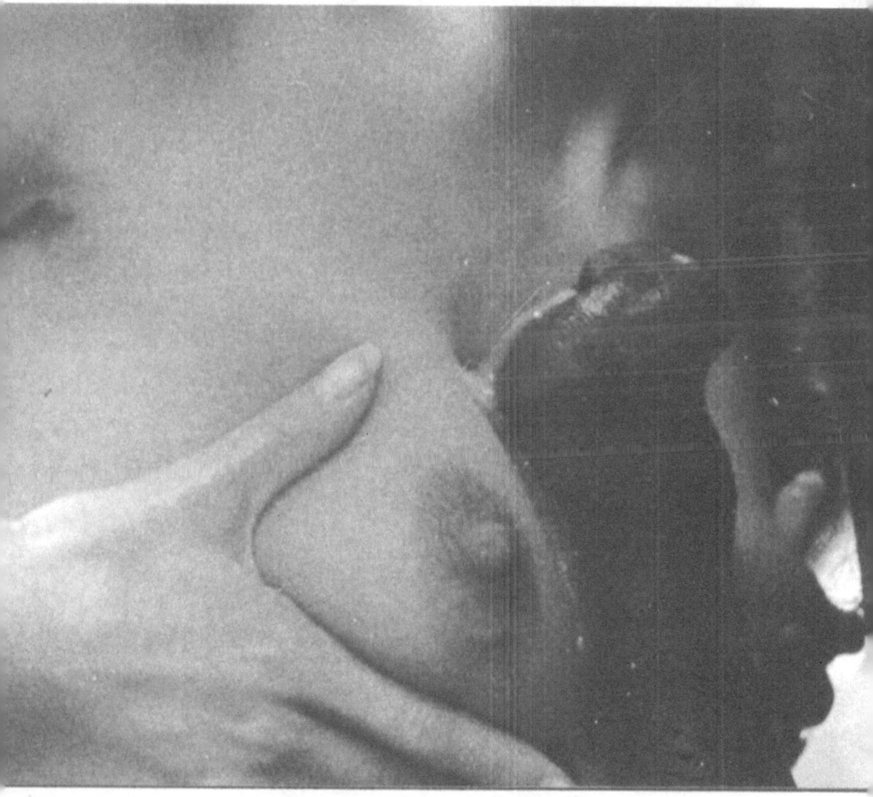

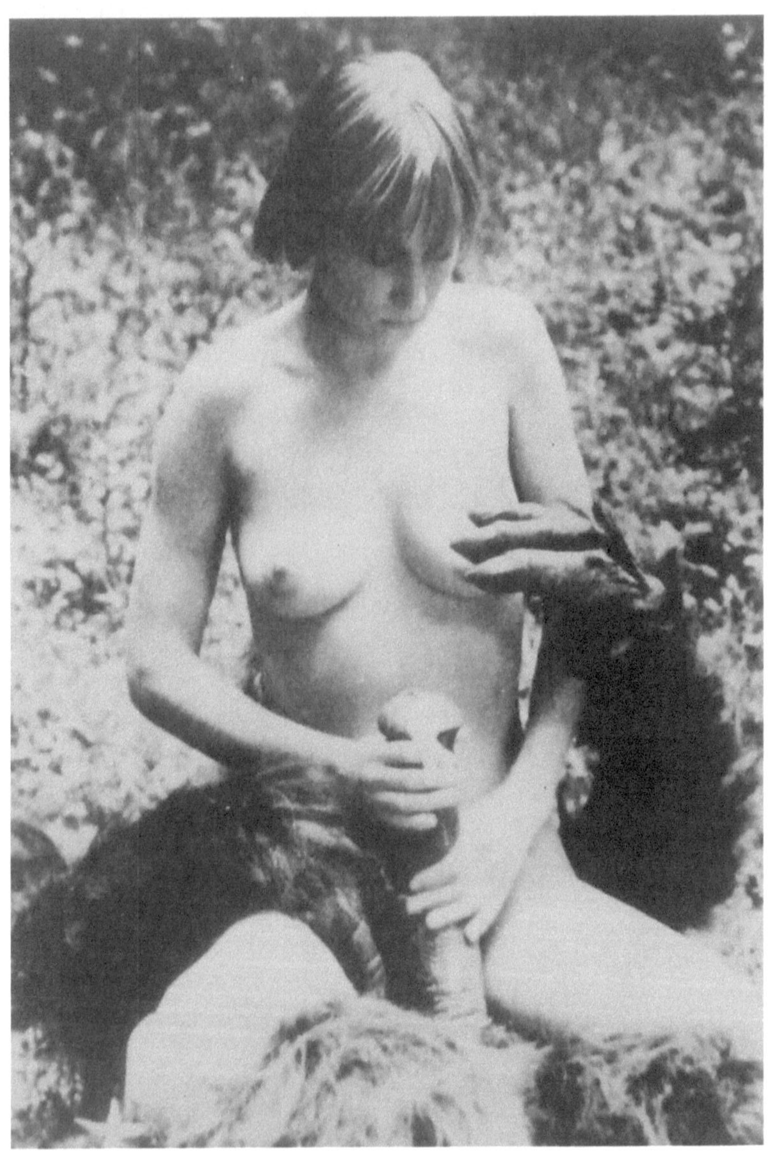

A naked young woman, a beast, a forest and an enormous cock:
it could only be Walerian Borowczyk's The Beast (1975)

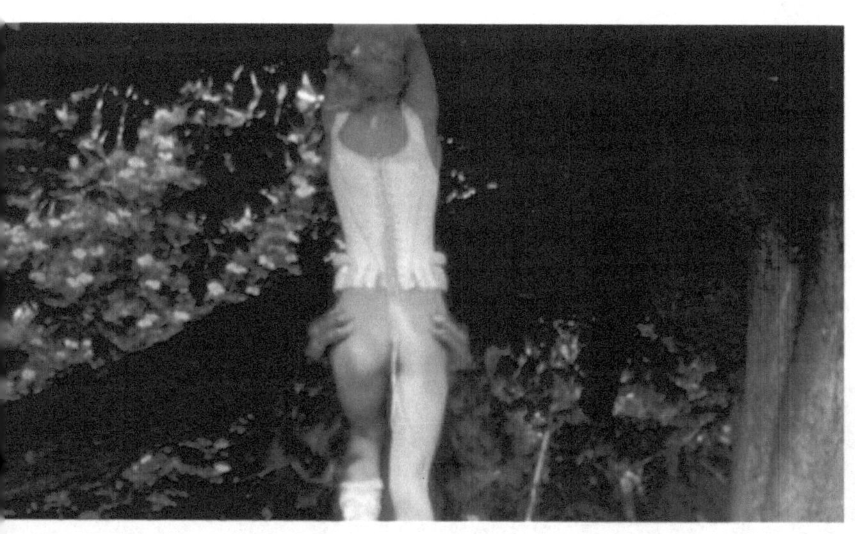

Beauty and the Beast, Borowczyk-style.

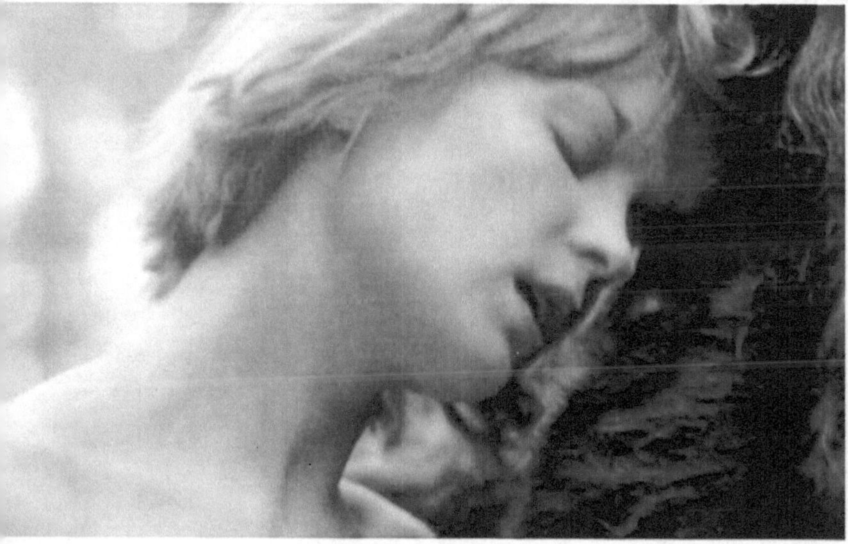

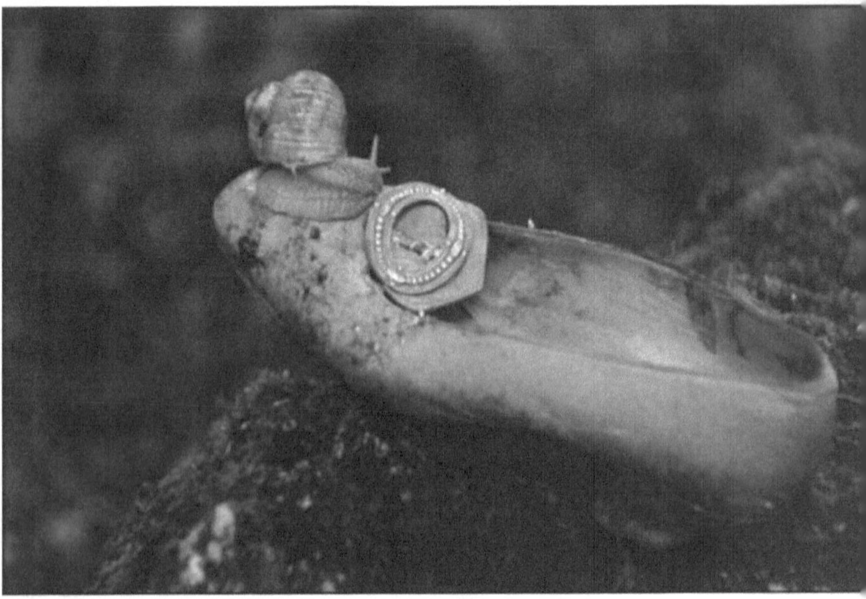

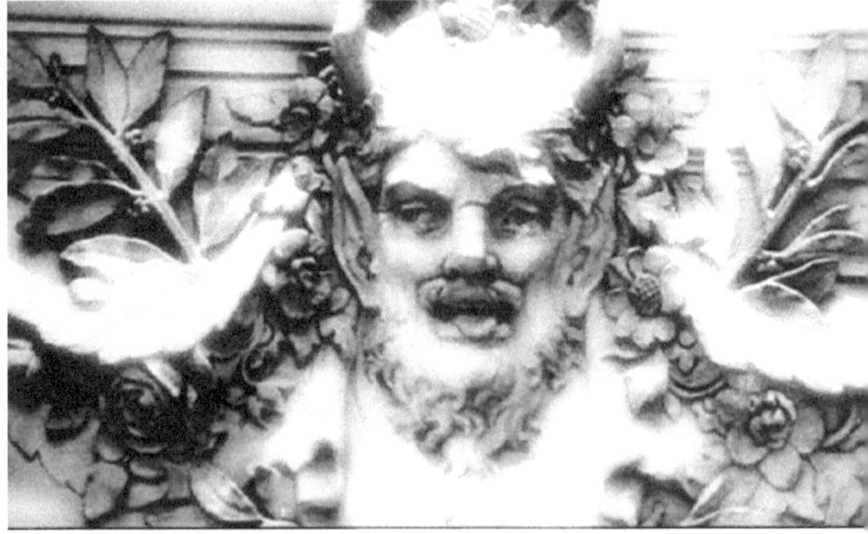

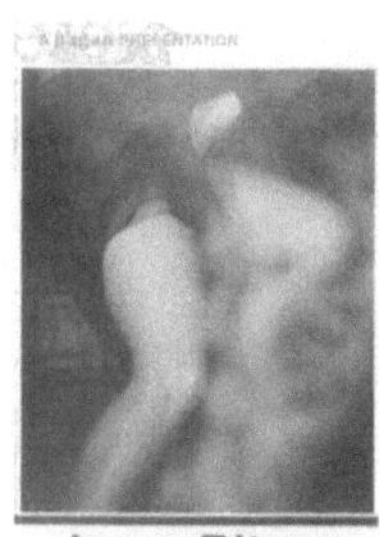

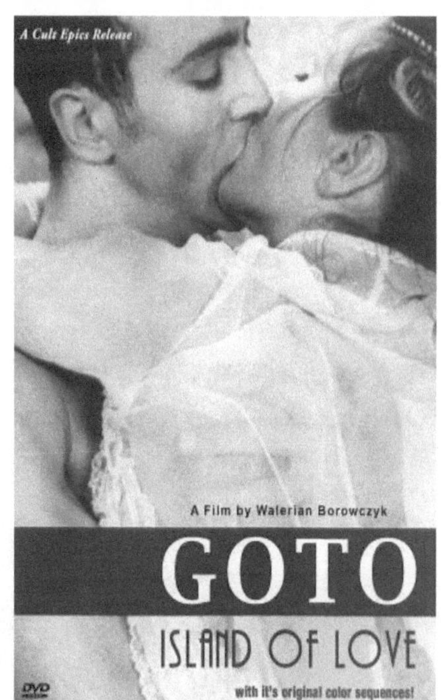

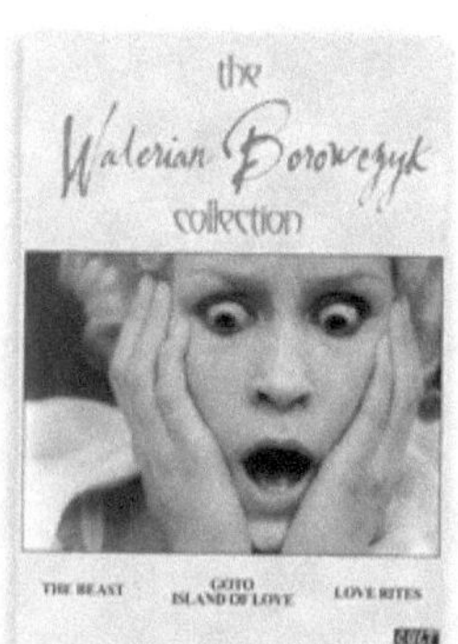

Some artwork from releases of
Walerian Borowczyk's movies

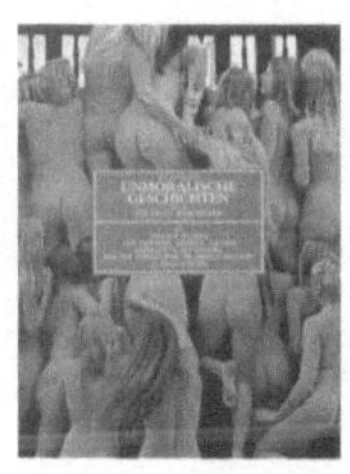

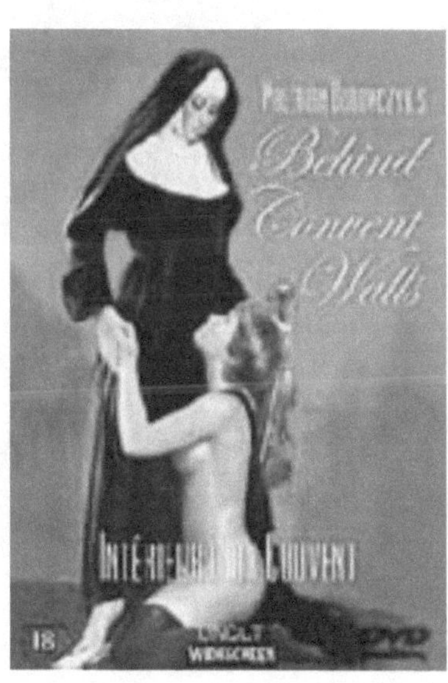

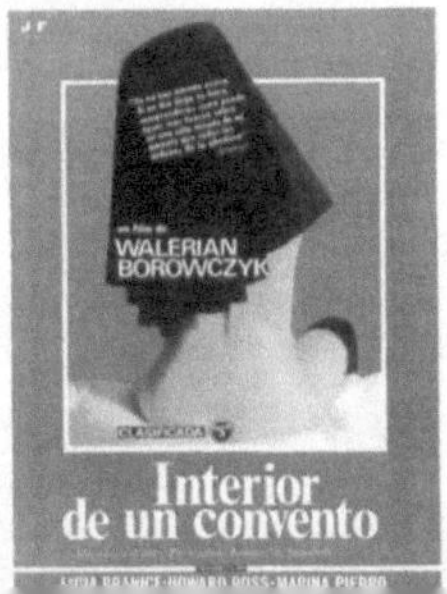

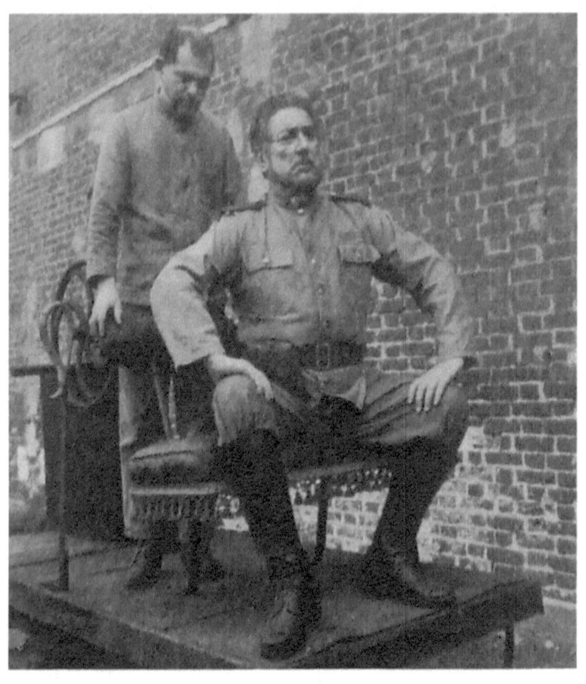

The king, Goto III, and his assassin, Grozo,
in a true masterpiece of cinema,
Walerian Borowczyk's Goto, Island of Love

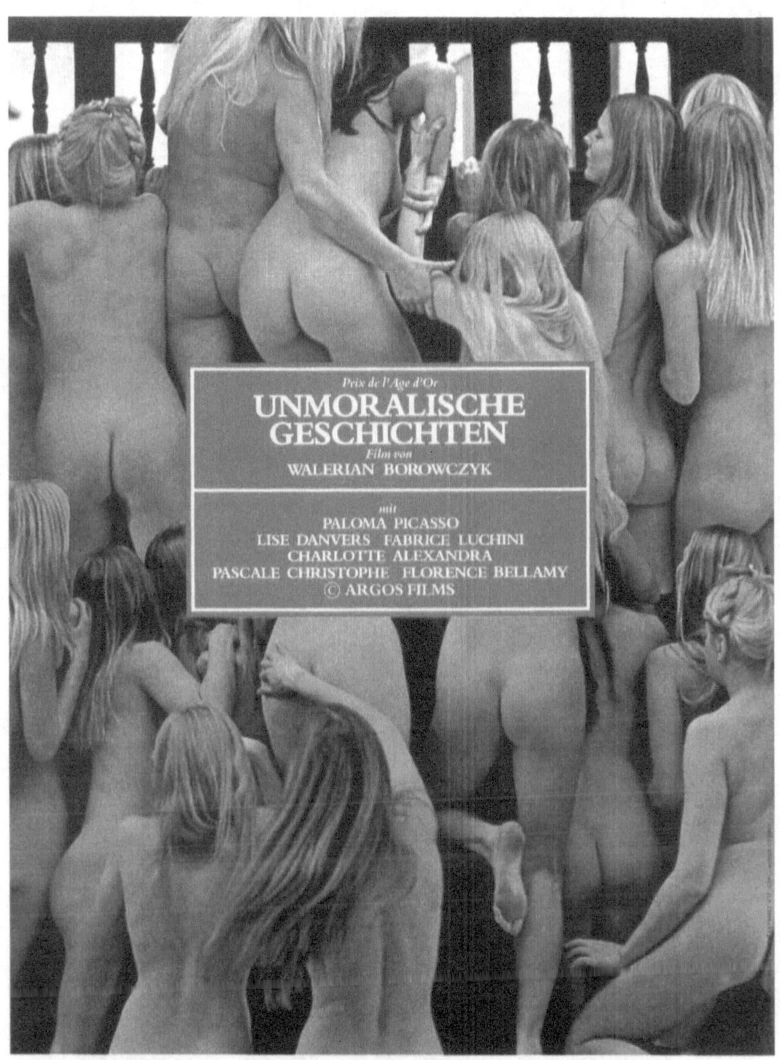

Argos Films' Immoral Tales

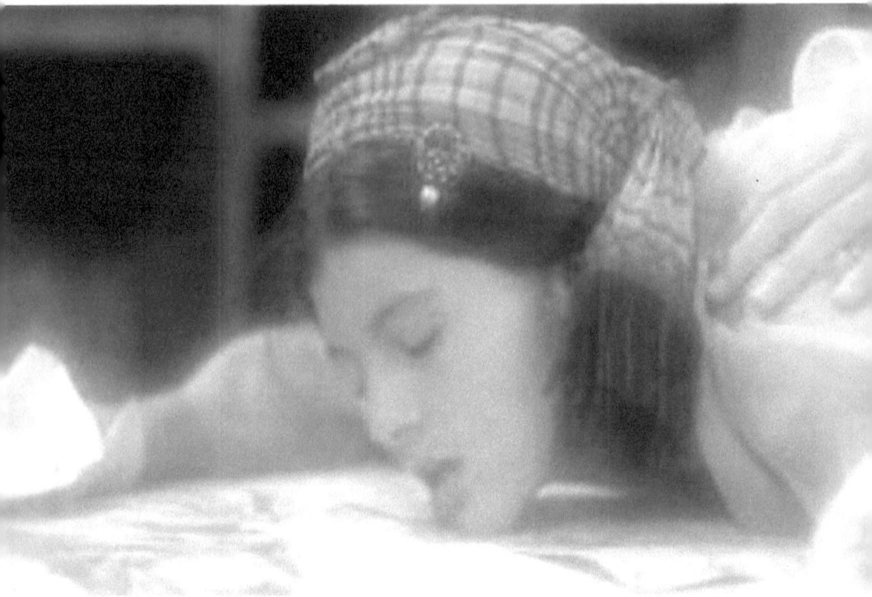

Three Immoral Women (above).
The Story of Sin (below).

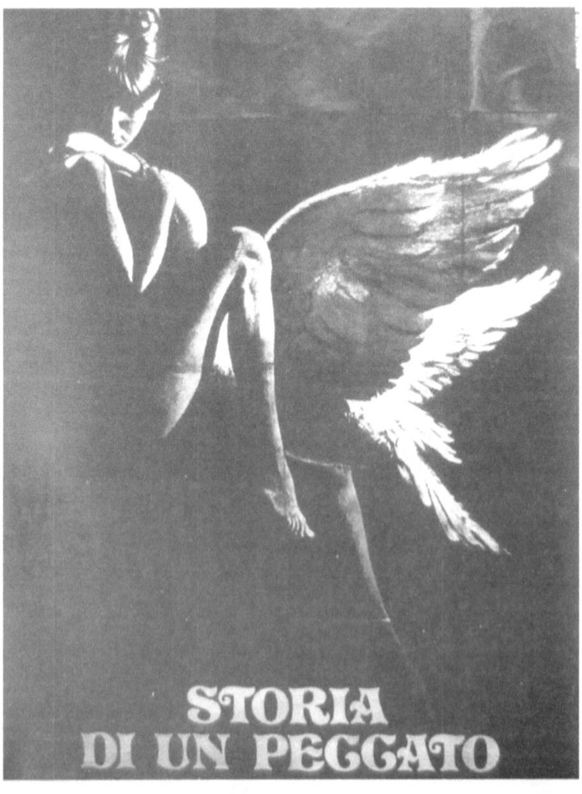

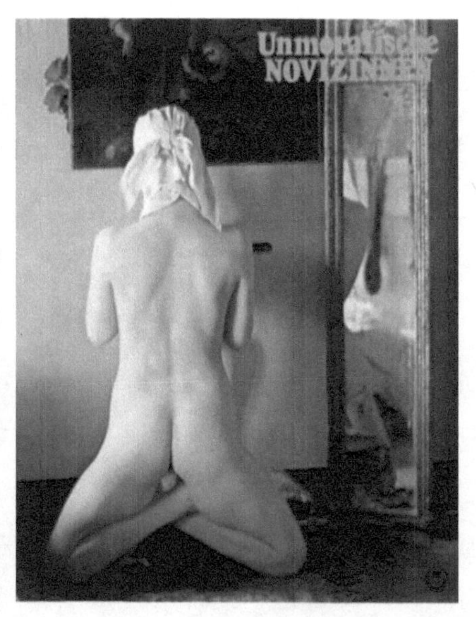

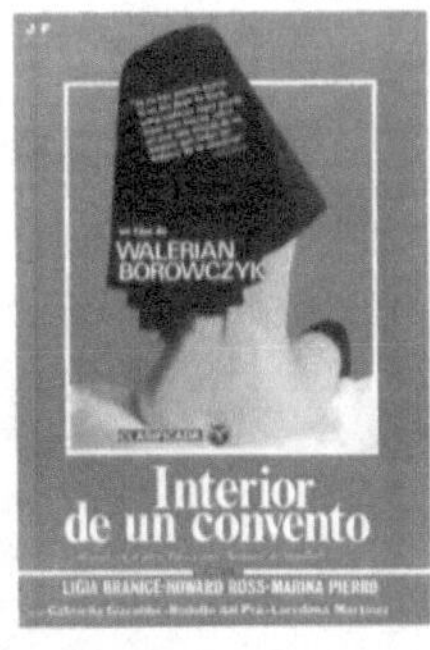

Behind Convent Walls (1977)

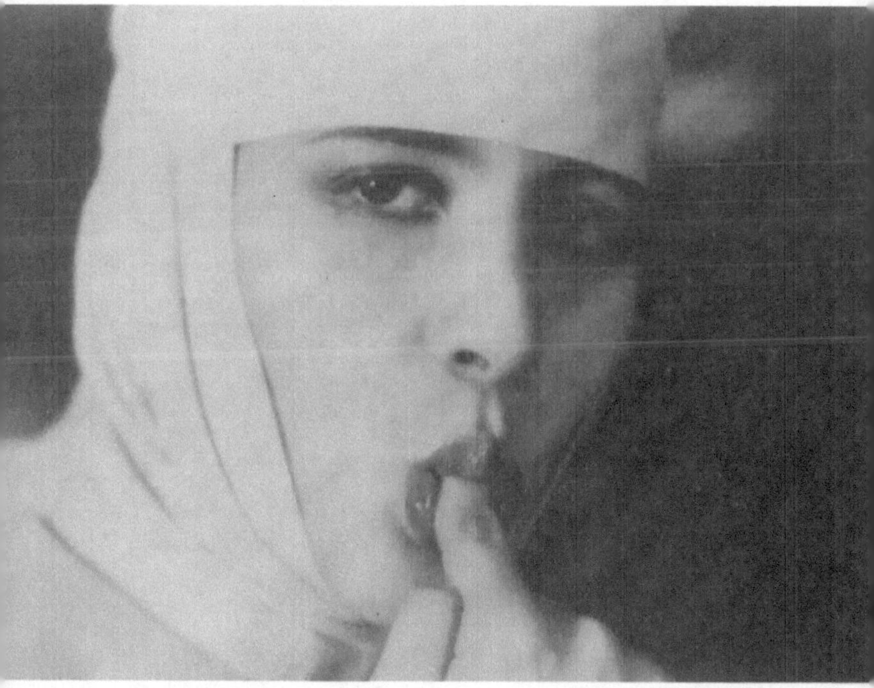

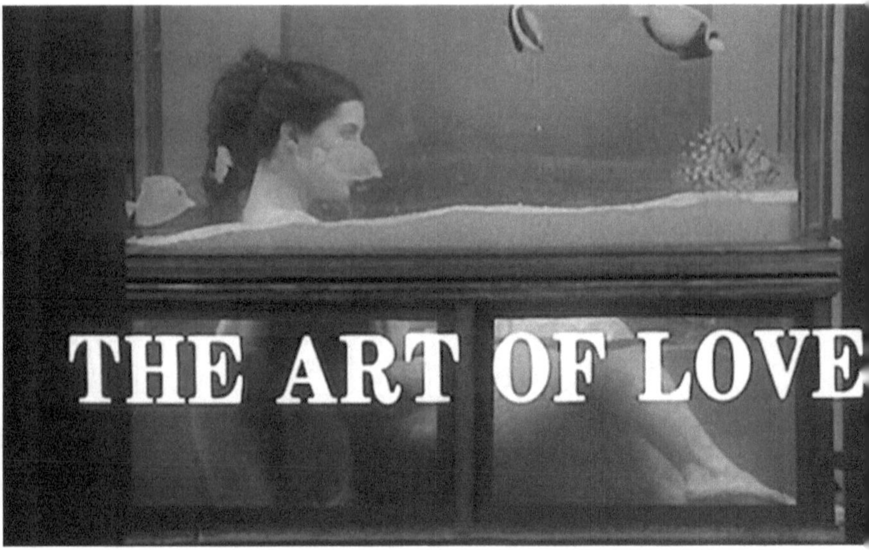

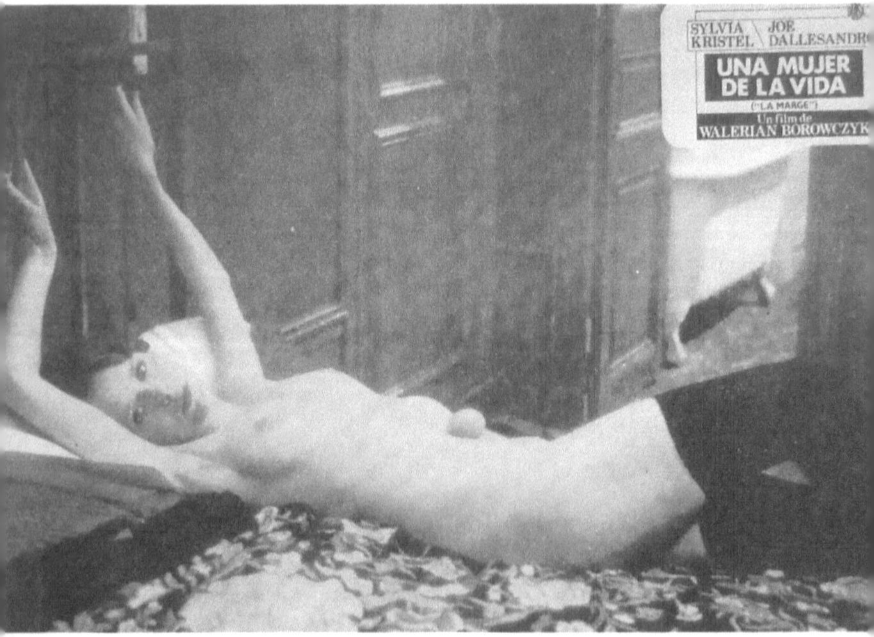

The Art of Love (top). La Marge (below).

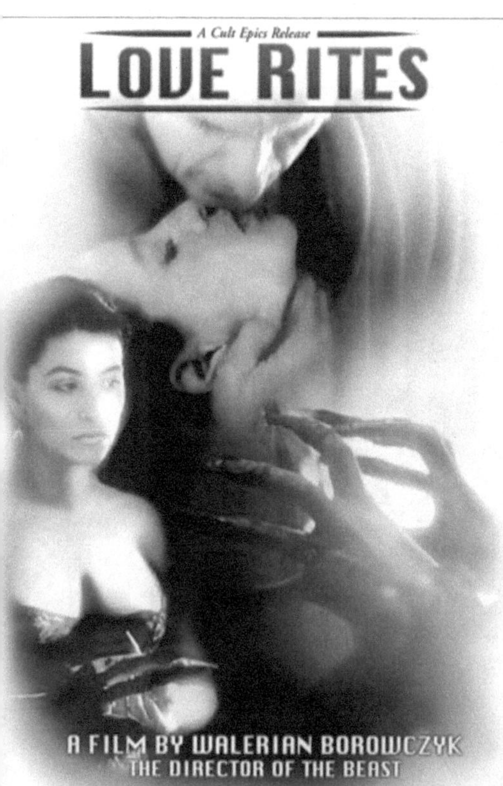

Two of the last movies directed by Borowczyk: a fine amour fou film, Love Rites, and easily his worst work, Emmanuelle 5.

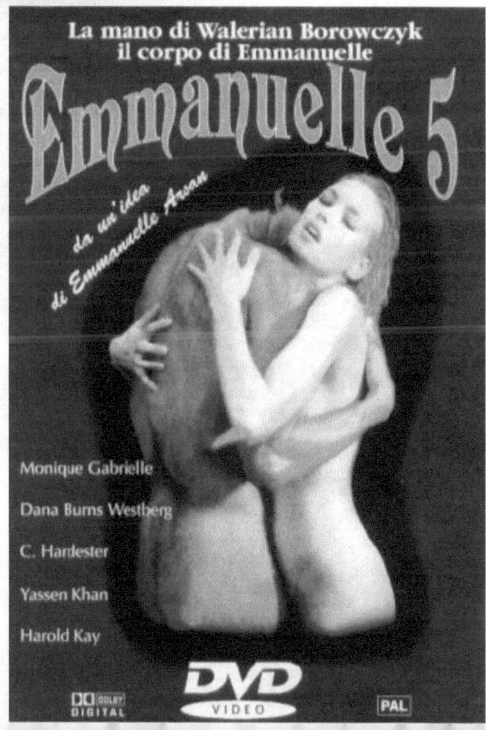

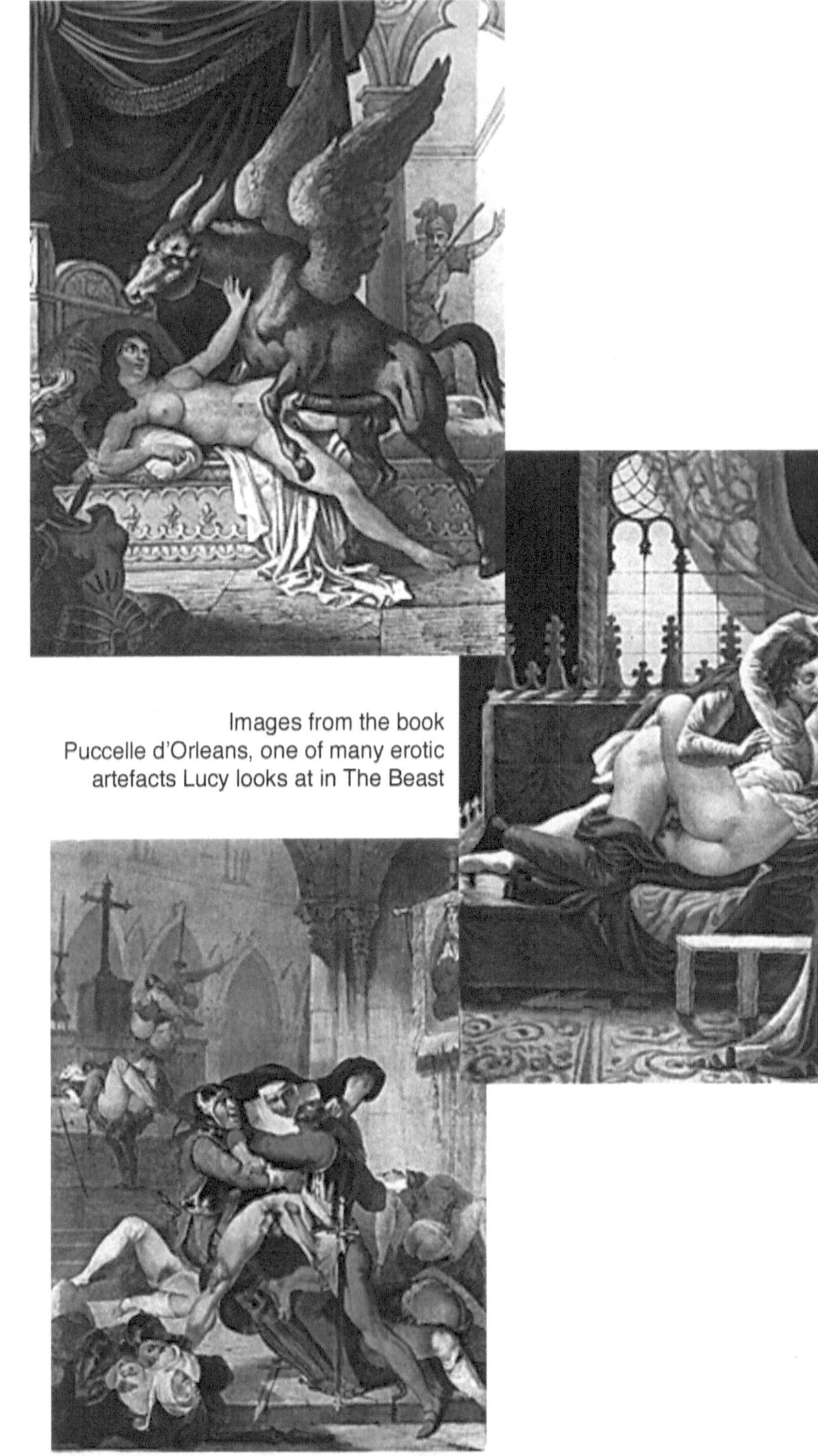

Images from the book
Puccelle d'Orleans, one of many erotic
artefacts Lucy looks at in The Beast

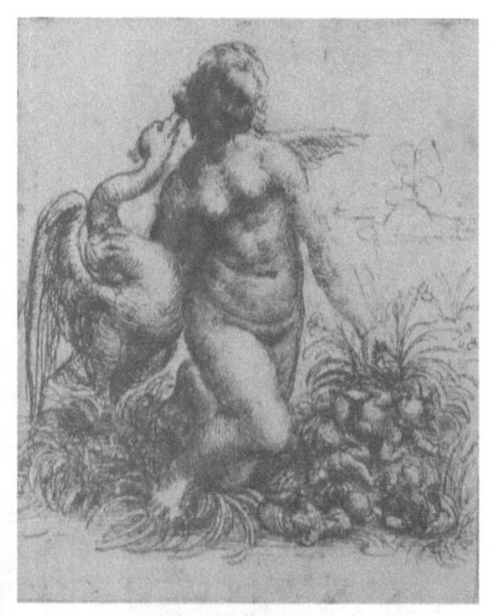

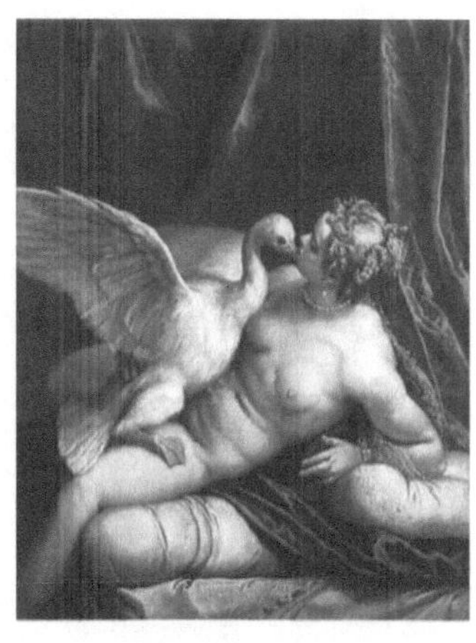

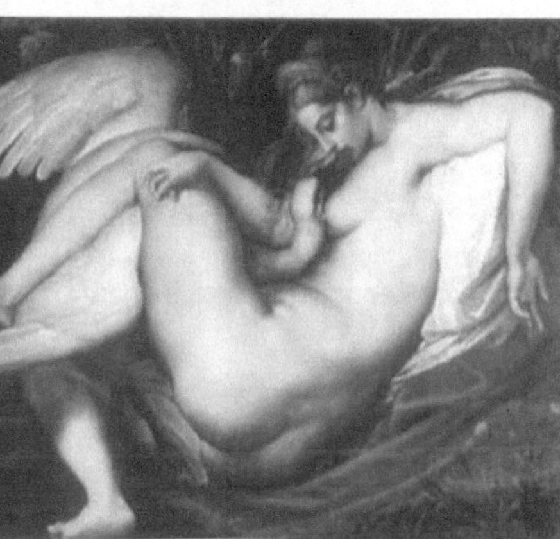

One of Walerian Borowczyk's favourite subjects in art, Leda and the Swan, which The Beast replays. Here are versions by Leonardo da Vinci, top, Veronese, top right. Peter Rubens, left, Giovanni Boldini, bottom left, and Luciano Castelli, below.

Asked who'd he like to be in history if he had the choice, Borowczyk said: 'if I have to choose an epoch and an identity, it would be that of Leda's swan in antiquity (if she really was as beautiful as the artists represent her)'.

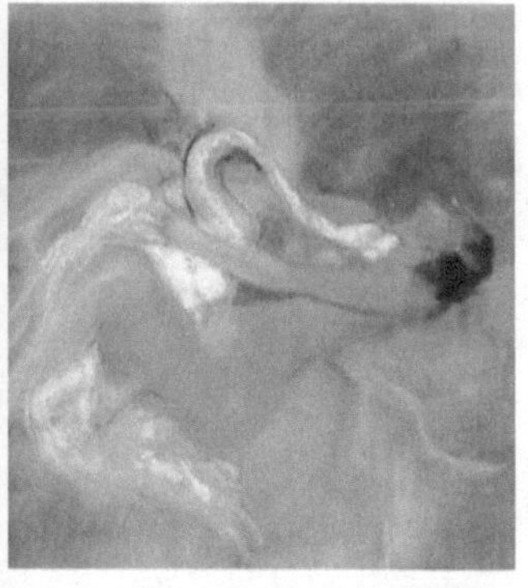

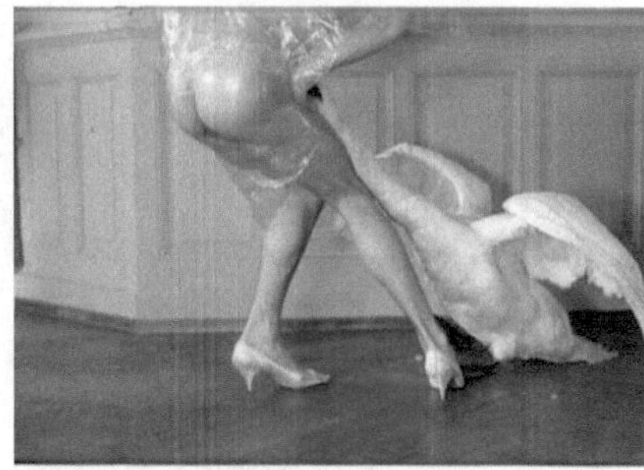

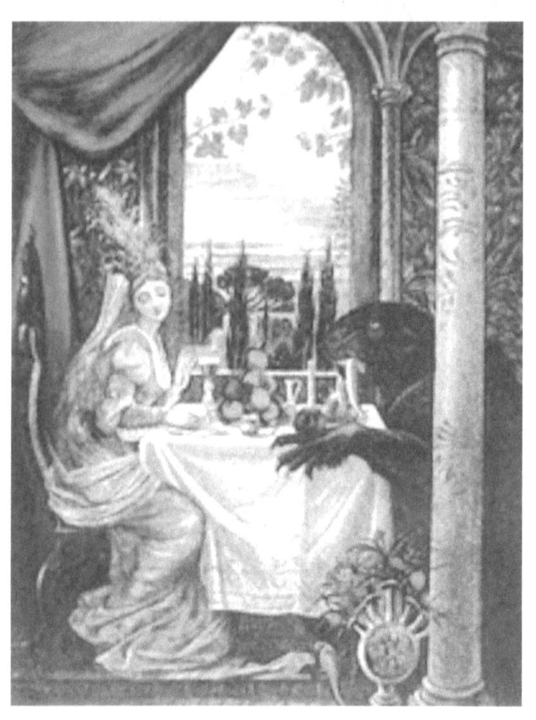

Beauty and the Beast by Mme Leprince de Beaumont, illustrations by Eleanor Vera Boyle

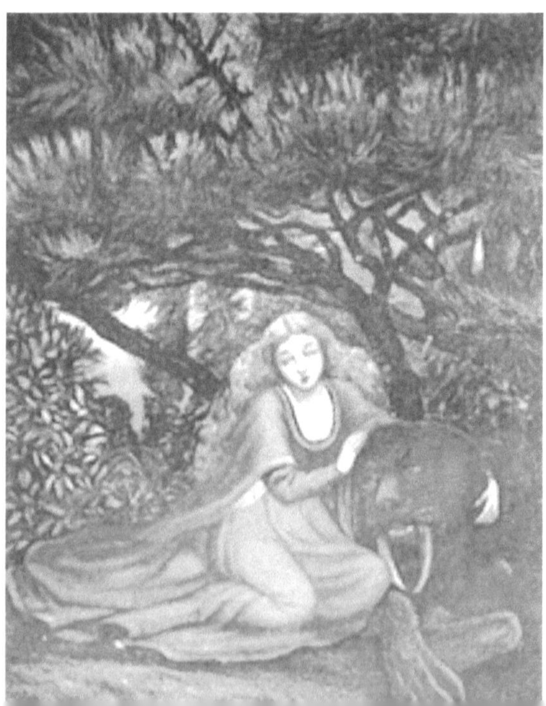

FOR THE FIRST TIME IN THEATRES IN 3D

Disney

Beauty and the Beast 3D

JANUARY 13

LIMITED THEATRICAL ENGAGEMENT

real D 3D

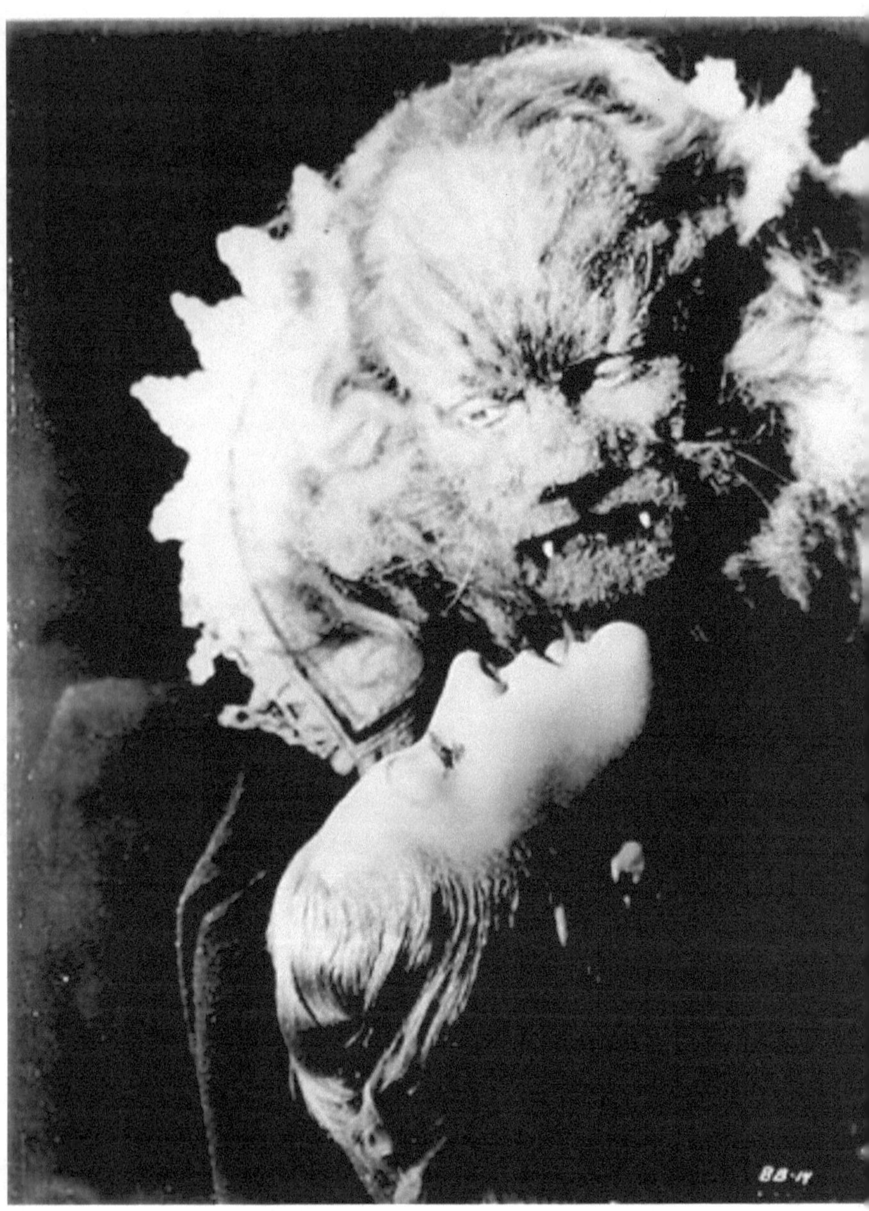

La Belle et La Bête (1945)

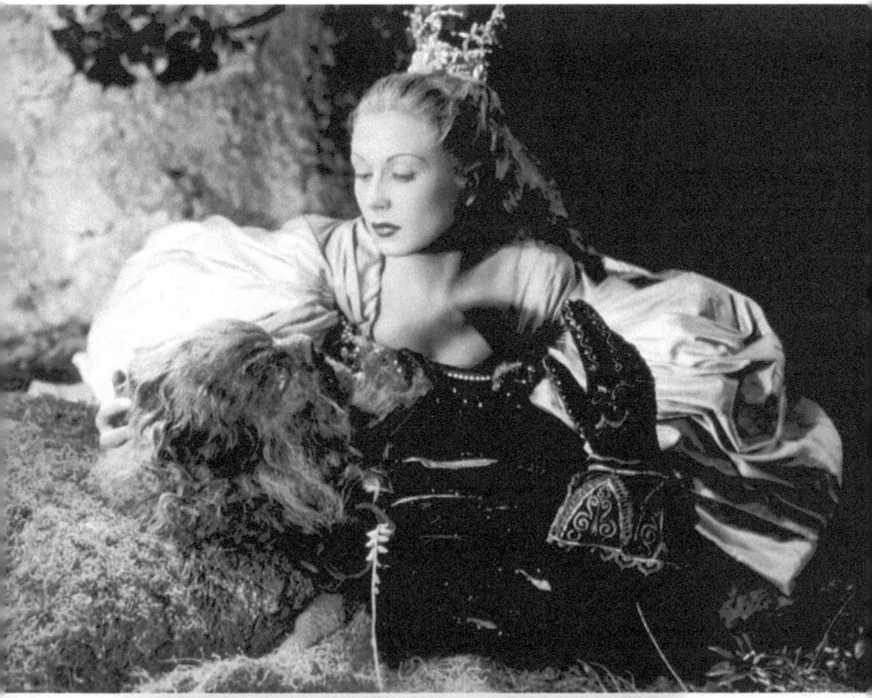

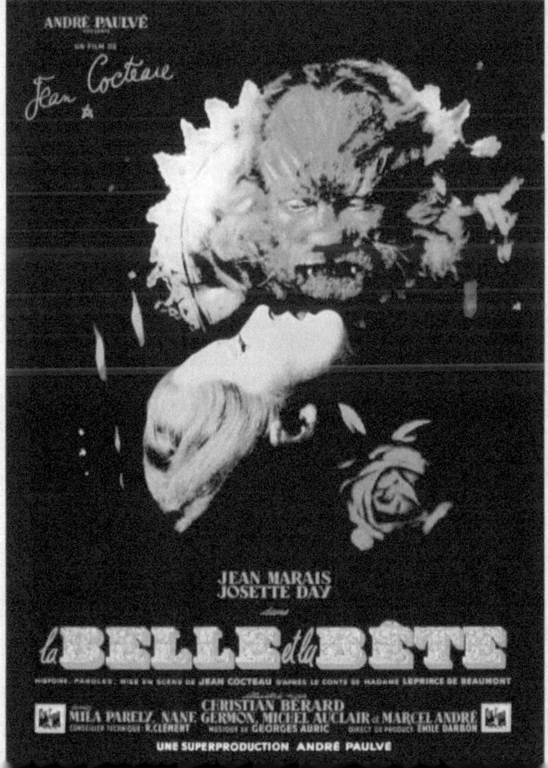

ANDRÉ PAULVÉ
UN FILM DE
Jean Cocteau
JEAN MARAIS
JOSETTE DAY
la BELLE et la BÊTE
HISTOIRE, PAROLES, MISE EN SCÈNE DE JEAN COCTEAU D'APRÈS LE CONTE DE MADAME LEPRINCE DE BEAUMONT
CHRISTIAN BERARD
MILA PARELY, NANE GERMON, MICHEL AUCLAIR et MARCEL ANDRÉ
CONSEILLER TECHNIQUE R.CLÉMENT
MUSIQUE DE GEORGES AURIC
DIRECT DE PRODUCT. EMILE DARBON
UNE SUPERPRODUCTION ANDRÉ PAULVÉ

2

LA BÊTE (THE BEAST)

AN EROTIC FAIRY TALE

'Dear Beast, you shall not die,' said Beauty, 'you shall live and become my husband. Here and now I offer you my hand, and swear that I will marry none but you. Alas, I fancied I felt only friendship for you, but the sorrow I have experienced clearly proves to me that I cannot live without you.'

Beauty had scare uttered these words when the castle became ablaze with lights before her eyes: fireworks, music – all proclaimed a feast. But these splendours were lost on her: she turned to her dear Beast, still trembling for his danger.

Judge of her surprise now! At her feet she saw no longer the Beast, who had disappeared, but a prince, more beautiful than Love himself, who thanked her for having put an end to his enchantment.

Charles Perrault, *Beauty and the Beast*[1]

Let me tell you what this business is about. It's cunt and horses!

Harry Cohn (head of Columbia Pictures)

1 C. Perrault, *Complete Fairy Tales*, Kestrel Books, London, 1962, 132.

The story of *La Bête* (a.k.a. *The Beast, The Beast in Heat* and *Death's Ecstasy*, 1975) involves an American heiress Lucy Broadhurst[2] (Lisbeth Hummel) being brought to a French chateau with her aunt Virginia (Elisabeth Kaza) by the scheming owners (in particular the marquis, Pierre de l'Esperance [played by Guy Tréjan]), who need to marry her to the earthy, degenerate (and somewhat backward) son of the family Mathurin (Pierre Benedetti) in order to circumvent a will which'll keep the family home intact.

That's the framing story, about grasping aristocrats, decadent morality, degenerate priests and sexually repressed young women.[3] This part of the film's set in the 20th century, though it's not the conventional modern, urban world of most movies. *La Bête* takes place exclusively at the French chateau and its grounds (the film is in French, but there is English dialogue – Virginia, Lucy and their chauffeur speak English).

There are subplots woven into the main narrative of *The Beast* of the imminent marriage of Lucy and Mathurin: the Cardinal de Balo, brother of the marquis's uncle, the disabled Duc de Balo (Marcel Dalio), who's supposed to come to the chateau to perform the wedding ceremony, but has fallen out with him;[4] the telephone calls to the Vatican, trying to persuade him to visit; the marquis, Pierre de l'Esperance, who's orchestrating the

2 Lucy is young, blonde, and wears a huge, expensive fur coat. Lucy is depicted as a naïve, innocent soul.
3 Borowczyk said he had written *La Bête* in two days, and had the initial idea in a café (of course – he was living in Paris, cafés being crucibles of many a creative venture).
4 The marquis uses blackmail to persuade the duke to ask his brother the cardinal to come to bless the marriage (the marquis claims that the duke poisoned his wife).

marriage, the uncouth Mathurin, who's happiest outside with his horses and is terrified of being married off (he has a bandaged hand, which's part of his beast nature); the priest (Roland Armontel) with his pretty choirboys who follow him around meekly (one is called Modeste, played by Thierry Bourdone);[5] the black man servant Ifany (Hassane Fall) who sneaks off to tup the marquis's daughter, Clarisse de l'Esperance (Pascale Rivault); and two children, friends of the marquis's daughter, who've come to witness the wedding.

You'll notice just how masculine (and patriarchal, and conventional) the set-up is at the chateau: there are no significant female characters until Lucy and her aunt show up (so the mare in the opening sequence is about the only feminine presence). Meanwhile, the rather prissy, fussy marquis is feminized (he wears aprons, he dusts, cleans and shaves Mathurin). And his uncle, the duke, is misogynistic (according to the marquis, he poisoned his wife).

But it's also the marquis who is leading the drama in the first act of *La Bête*, and up until Lucy has her erotic dream of the beast (after which, Lucy and Romilda take over as the main protagonists). It's the marquis who arranges the marriage, who cajoles de Balo to contact his brother the cardinal, who cleans up Mathurin, and writes love letters to Lucy.

In *The Beast*, marriage and finding a mate is for the declining aristocracy an economic necessity – the estate of the chateau is falling apart. The de l'Esperances need

5 It's the choirboys who play the harpsichord, which justifies the use of the music within the movie.

this marriage; they need the American heiress's $$$$. It's patriarchy's marriage of economics – money, not love. But *The Beast* is no Marxist treatise, it's a Freudian-Surrealist-psychoanalytical take on Western marriage.

The other main narrative in *The Beast* depicts Lucy's masturbatory fantasies of erotic encounters with a beast in a sunlit forest, set in the 18th century, imagining herself as Romilda de l'Esperance (played by Sirpa Lane, 1951-99),[6] one of the ancestors of the marquis's family, meeting the legendary beast that has haunted the family for centuries (the legend is that a beast emerges every two hundreds years in the park).

Walerian Borowczyk, 53 when it was released, called *The Beast* 'really more of a comedy than an erotic film'. Let that prepare you for this extraordinary movie. Because the central section, the fairy tale sequence of the beast pursuing and fucking a woman, is meant to be very silly, very over-the-top, very unbelievable. *The Beast is* a comedy, and it *is* erotic. And it's so completely mad you can't help but be swept along by it. Have a look at some of the comments on the Internet Movie Database and Amazon.com for some funny takes on the movie.

It's not *Hill Street Blues, Friends* or *Avatar*, it's *European*, utterly non-American and un-American.[7] Every question about *The Beast* can be answered by the statement: *it's a comedy.*

Walerian Borowczyk remarked that:

---

6 Sirpa Lane had a short career before she died of AIDS in 1999. *The Beast* was her third or fourth movie, and most of her work was in exploitation or underground cinema. She was 24 when *The Beast* was filmed.

7 The 'American heiress' in the movie, Lucy Broadhurst, is played by a Danish actress speaking in French and not very American English.

> *La Bête* is a fantasy film and especially an 'adult film'. But first of all it is a film about dream mechanisms. Dreams translate our deepest desires. Why then cover with a veil of silence the temptation of an intimate relationship with an animal? (J. Gerber, 169)

Walerian Borowczyk here outlines one of his central goals – which is to make manifest desires and fears that are hidden or suppressed (he's especially fond of exposing them within a religious/ Catholic context, partly because the desires, when they erupt, appear even more outrageous. Organized religion is a great environment against which to set explosions of desire).

Among the crew on *La Bête* were DPs Bernard Daillencourt and Marcel Grignon, Noël Véry, camera operator, Jacques D'Ovidio, production designer, set decorator Alain Guillé, wardrobe by Piet Bolscher, make-up by Odette Berroyer, production manager Dominique Duvergé and sound by Michel Laurent and Jean-Pierre Ruh (sound mixer was Alex Pront). No less than six assistant editors are credited (Alain Cayrade, Florence Dauman, Claude Delon, Jean-Pierre Platel, Monique Prim and Michel Valio – some were trainées), but it's Boro who has the main editing credit. Much credit should go to producer Anatole Dauman for backing this OTT movie. Many on the team were Borowczyk regulars.

It's unlikely that you will recognize any of the performers in *The Beast*: Sirpa Lane, Lisbeth Hummel, Elisabeth Kaza, Guy Tréjan, Pierre Benedetti, Roland Armontel, Pascale Rivault, Robert Capia, etc.

A short film, *Une Collection Particulière* (1973), a

catalogue and documentary of Walerian Borowczyk's own collection of erotica, was going to be part of *Immoral Tales*, as well as *The Beast* (it was narrated by and starred André Pieyre de Mandiargues). *Une Collection Particulière* is an amusing and playful exploration of a host of erotica, including sex toys, dildoes, prints, photographs, and paintings. There are some early devices designed to titillate – wooden models and automata (such as a policeman getting an erection, a man fucking a donkey (echoes of *The Beast*!), and strip shows and silhouettes of people tupping). These quaint machines pre-date cinema, but simulate movement and life, being part of Borowczyk's fascination with animation, and animating the inanimate, which was such a large part of Borowczyk's early films.

The 'controversy' surrounding *The Beast* from its release onwards pivoted on the fantasy scenes of Romilda de l'Esperance having sex with 'the beast'. There were the inevitable run-ins with censors and the media. *La Bête* retained its power to upset viewers, even shock, many years later. In the U.K., the British Board of Film Classification could not pass it; in 1978 it was granted an 'X' by the Greater London Council (and only after extensive cuts), and only allowed to be seen in London. It was not granted a certificate by the BBFC in Britain until 2001, due to the relaxation of censorship laws, turning up on video, DVD and the FilmFour channel.

⚜

The very first shot of *The Beast* is of Mathurin, the beast's incarnation in the present day; the second shot is a C.U. of a horse's cock. *La Bête* doesn't mess about: it begins with a copulation scene, complete with erection, vagina and penetration shots, of two horses in the courtyard outside some stables.[8] The graphic scene's covered with a rapid montage of long lens images of the horses' bodies, which are always in motion, the male moving restlessly around the female. There are close-ups of the horses' genitals (the stallion's penis distended, the mare's vagina opening and closing, with squelchy sound effects), accompanied by loud snorts and the clatter of hooves (the echoey sounds of the horses are heard over the titles too: *The Beast* opens, in fact, with loud horse sounds, with the titles in white over black; the main title is in red, aptly. And there is a quotation from Voltaire at the top of the movie).

The explicit imagery of copulating animals sets up the central erotic encounter of the film, between Lucy Broadhurst/ Romilda de l'Esperance and the beast, when Lucy and her aunt Virginia arrive at the stables in their limo (as if Lucy and Mathurin are simply animals being bred, exploited for the needs of the humans). Immediately, Lucy gets out of the vehicle and starts taking Polaroids of the horses (a simple device to illustrate her sexual curiosity, which makes her *dopplegänger*, Romilda, venture out into the forest. Lucy now has a startling close-up of the horses copulating – a great commercial for Polaroid cameras!). In the car, Virginia had responded to Lucy's enthusiastic praise of 'beautiful France': 'beautiful France has always lived in lust'.

8 While an action or adventure movie might open with a short piece of action, it's typical for a Walerian Borowczyk picture, that's all about erotic desire, to open with a copulation scene!

The Beast does take a while to get going after that extraordinary opening sequence (one of the strangest in cinema history. *Terms of Endearment* or *Great Expectations* this ain't). There's a bunch of characters to introduce, and their relationships.[9] There's a lot of not very distinctive talk, but in the midst of it all (around ten or so minutes), Borowczyk is slipping in numerous details – such as a snail crawling on the duke's hand (snails crop up many times in *The Beast*), or the painting of Romilda, which crops up many times (and was likely another Borowczyk creation). And the marquis and the duke have an ambiguous relationship (the marquis seems to keep his uncle locked up – he is forever locking and unlocking doors like Bluebeard in the fairy tale, as if he's always got something to hide. That the duke is ill and in a wheelchair needs no gloss).

Horses also crop up in Boro's first feature, *Goto – Island of Love*. In that 1968 picture,[10] there is a classic romp in the hay between the heroine, Glossia, and her soldier lover Gono in the stables. But Walerian Borowczyk's reference in *Goto*, or the kind of sex romp he's thinking of, is not taken, as with *The Beast*, from cinema, but much further back: Borowczyk is a connoisseur of pornography and erotic literature – he is

9 Walerian Borowczyk's movies simply dispense with cinematic devices that act as lead-ins or set-ups that convent-ional movies employ. In a word: exposition. He simply expects the audience to work a little and keep up. That's quite common in the European art film, though (however, in *The Beast*, exposition does weigh down the first act of the picture).

In Walerian Borowczyk's cinema, everything in the picture has a function – in particular his art direction, which's second to none: the objects, the furniture, the animals, the lighting, the scenery, the people, and those fabulous costumes.

10 *Goto: Island of Love* opens with shots of the stables, and horses exercising.

referencing erotic art of the 17th and 18th centuries, in written as well as painted or drawn form. *Goto* knows that it's a cliché, well-worn like an old boot, to portray lovers tupping in the hay in the stables, but it's not a cliché from the history of *cinema*, but from the history of *literature.*[11]

In other words, when you're looking at a Walerian Borowczyk picture, you have to think in terms of literature and graphic art (painting, drawing, printmaking) going back centuries, not only to cinema as an artform with its roots in silent films from the early 1900s. Before erotic cinema there was erotic photography, for instance.[12]

As soon as the 1975 film cuts to Lucy and her aunt Virginia in the car, the film begins to gel: you know that something more interesting's going to happen with Lucy around – the marquis, the duke, Mathurin and the curé are rather unappealing characters. And all of that stuff about grooming Mathurin so he'll be presentable to meet Lucy is not particularly engaging. And notice how Walerian Borowczyk has Lucy play the character in her mid-teens here, rather than the 22 years-old that actress Lisbeth Hummel actually is.[13] Lucy is excitedly talking

11 And in numerous erotic prints – such as by Jean-Honoré Fragonard, Thomas Rowlandson, Johan Tobias Sergel, etc.
12 There is some superb French photographic erotica, which Borowczyk has sometimes used in his films, dating from the 1900s-1910s. And before that erotic literature, and erotic prints, and so on and on.
13 Hummel was born in 1952, in Copenhagen; aside from *The Beast*, she hasn't appeared in many other films. She has done photos for softcore porn magazines. Finding Lucy and Romilda would have been the toughest job: ideally, Lucy and Romilda should be younger – 17, say, but finding an actress who can play and look 17 and also agree to do what they have to do isn't easy.

about the world outside as they drive through it. And then, to emphasis the fairy tale nature of this movie, she jumps out of the car and disappears into the forest. The chateau is culture, sanctuary, safety, and the forest is danger, mystery, the unknown – and desire. By having Lucy stop here and run off into the forest, Borowczyk alludes to any number of fairy tales (yet this woodland is also full of sunlight and trilling birdsong).

He's also announcing: folks, this isn't going to be your usual film. One of the ways he does that is to have really strange things popping up. In the forest, in the lake, there appears to be a body under the water (or Romilda's corset, or perhaps Romilda herself), the bubbles audible as they pop up. Truly weird, partly because it doesn't link up with much else in the picture (except the repeated images of Romilda's corset in the lake. Is it the beast? Is it Romilda's dead-alive corpse?).

La Bête incorporates characters and situations straight out of an 18th century comedy of manners, or French farce, or 19th century erotica: the randy, aged curé with his two beautiful youths, the black man servant who fucks the marquis's daughter, the town girl who wanders into a forest and is raped by a man-beast (she hates it at first, then enjoys it).

People are constantly caught in mid-tup, mid-grope, mid-day-dream in *La Bête*. Clarisse de l'Esperance and the black servant Ifany are always disturbed when they get freaky (and of course it's always the head of the house, and Clarisse's father, who disturbs them – pure Sigmund Freud), and Lucy's masturbatory fantasies are interrupted.

La Bête was classic Walerian Borowczyk, with all of his favourite motifs and themes on display: an incredible sense of detail (a snail on a shoe); a painterly sense of colour,[14] light, and space; an elegant olde worlde setting (a French chateau); high art allusions (to, for instance, painting); and a pounding Domenico Scarlatti harpsichord soundtrack.

Oh, and there's lots of sex: erotic prints (one shows a winged horse entering a woman,[15] which ties in with the bestiality theme - see below); erotic photographs; close-ups of women's naked torsos through semi-transparent gowns; women masturbating; people fucking; and, most controversially, the beast fucking a woman.

The chateau and its pretty landscaped surroundings are perfectly 18th century, drawing on the art of Jean-Antoine Watteau, François Boucher and Jean-Honoré Fragonard. Inside the house, Lucy asks de Balo about ghost stories; he shows her a book of leaves and miscellanea that Romilda collected in the forest; he also shows her the white corset of Romilda's in a cabinet, which has claw marks on it (it's typical of Borowczyk that one of the symbolic or fetishized objects in *The Beas* should be a corset!).

One of the sources of *La Bête* was an 18th century French fable, *La veritable histoire de la bête de Gevaudin* (which Walerian Borowczyk had turned into an 18

14 Red is the predominant symbolic colour in this contemporary erotic fairy tale - the red rose, blood, and the bright red walls in the chateau.
15 This is taken from *Puccelle D'Orléans*. The book was probably chosen partly for its illustration of sex between a woman and a winged horse. That it's a spoof by Voltaire about Joan of Arc adds to the themes (identifying Lucy with Jeanne d'Arc).

minute short in 1973, entitled *La véritable histoire de la bête du Gévaudan*; it was shown as a work-in-progress at the London Film Festival, comprising the last of three self-contained films in *Immoral Tales*). Another was a movie that Borowczyk was hired to work on, Alain Fleischer's *Les rendezvous en forêt*. Producer Anatole Dauman wanted Borowczyk to spice up the ending, and Borowczyk constructed a beast suit.[16] However, Fleischer prevented Borowczyk from adding to *Les rendezvous en forêt* through legal action, and Borowczyk would later use his beast costume in *La Bête*. *La Bête* also, unlike too many of Borowczyk's other films, is not dubbed (or a large proportion of the movie has source sound). There's a much greater sense of performance and atmosphere.

Walerian Borowczyk and his team set up classic oppositions: the house and the forest; inside and outside; the dark rooms, with the windows always shuttered (even during the day),[17] and the bright, sunlit woodland; repressed sexuality inside and unbridled lust outside; paganism vs. Catholicism. The interiors, richly furnished, hint at blood, virginal or animal, with deep red predominating, and white and black also.

Clarisse de l'Esperance (who wears dreadlocks, boots and jeans and drives a 2CV when she's not naked, which's most of the time) tups the black man servant Ifany (he has a large pecker, of course). Their couplings are always interrupted by the master of the house yelling for his butler. When Ifany leaves, Clarisse resignedly

16 The beast has gorilla hands and a wolf head, and black hair all over. Borowczyk himself played the beast. Nah, just kidding.
17 The marquis closes the shutters, even tho' it's a pretty Spring day, as if he's shutting out the untameable natural world.

climbs onto the wooden end of the bed and rubs her clit to orgasm, the camera zooming in on her pubis (people are so horny in *The Beast*, that when their lovers leave, they carry on).[18] In one lengthy and striking sequence shot (it's striking how many lengthy sequence shots Walerian Borowczyk uses), Clarisse and Ifany are hard at it on the bed (Clarisse keeps her boots on, a nice fetishistic touch), when the marquis hollers for him. So the lovers break apart; the man climbs out of bed, his half-erect cock prominent, dresses, and leaves. Clarisse, frustrated, straddles the headboard to rub herself to orgasm. The camera trucks in slightly, reframing her body, concentrating on her cunt. But this isn't the end of an already lengthy take: Clarisse gives up and sits on the bed, then moves around the room, pulls on a dressing gown, then opens the wardrobe to let out the two young children brought for the wedding. And she's shut them up in a wardrobe so she can fuck Ifany! You won't see that in your average Hollywood movie. (Even sillier, at the end of the movie, when all of the characters appear as Lucy wakes them with her hysteria, Ifany and Clarisse emerge naked from the wardrobe, 'cos the kids Marie and Stéphane are sleeping on the bed!).

The tupping of Clarisse and Ifany brings in a racial element again: kisses across the racial divide had been seen in earlier movies, but for 1975 it was fairly unusual outside of porno seeing two naked people, one pale white, the other black, fucking each other (thirty years and more on, it's still very unusual).

18 Everybody is in a state of perpetual sexual desire in *The Beast*. Even the priest talks about it being Spring, evoking what animals get up to in Spring.

The ethnic angle is also noted by the black characters themselves – when Ifany goes out to the Rolls Royce and talks to the black (apparently American) chauffeur. Their dialogue includes allusions to slaves. Note also that the beast is black, and the women linked to the beast, Romilda and Lucy, are dressed in white. It's *Beauty and the Beast*, and it's *King Kong* too, with all the racial stereotyping of those stories.

Lucy's in an erotic limbo: she's been brought to the chateau to be married off to Mathurin, and exists in that vertiginous space in between singledom and marriage. Lucy spends much of her time mooning about on her own in her room, leaving the others, the aunt Virginia, the marquis Pierre de l'Esperance, his son Mathurin, the curé and the Duc de Balo, to scheme and plot.

When she's first seen alone, Lucy explores her room:[19] after looking at a painting of the Madonna and Child,[20] and some books (including a book of *Sermons*) – the Catholic/ Christian admonitions, she soon uncovers an erotic book in a wooden cabinet (after discarding a duller book).[21] It contains black-and-white drawings illustrating some erotic texts, a spoof by Voltaire of Joan of Arc, called *La Puccelle D'Orléans* (1789). There's even a shot of the title page, just so's the audience knows

---

19 Like Thérèse in *Immoral Tales*, Lucy looks round her room for something to entertain her; both women uncover erotica (which is never far from the surface of everyday life in Borowczyk Land).

20 As if reminding Lucy: this is what women are supposed to be like – demure and motherly yet also virginal, like the Virgin Mary.

21 Lucy's inquisitiveness also uncovers a drawing of a dog and a woman getting freaky on the back of a frame (once again, it looks as if Borowczyk has produced this sketch). It resembles the famous art of Hans Bellmer.

exactly what piece of 18th century erotica it is (no doubt the book – a rarity – was from Boro's own collection).

It's another erotic moment for Lucy, and because it's erotic she is inevitably disturbed by the black chauffeur bringing in her things (erotic films always have to put off fulfilment – i.e., orgasm – towards the end of the movie, in the same way that the big action set-piece only occurs in a conventional movie at the climax. In *The Beast*, the climax is literal – actually, it's multiple, too: Clarisse comes, Lucy comes, Romilda comes, and the Beast comes many times).

Later, Lucy masturbates while perusing the Polaroids she's taken of the copulating horses spread on her pillow (the DPs frame the shot for the delectation of the viewer, with Lucy's legs and buttocks turned towards the camera on the bed, Lucy pulling down her stockings and panties and pushing her fingers inside herself from behind.) The shot concentrates exclusively on Lucy's ass and fingers, with her face out of shot (also, it's a lengthy take, and there are no cuts to Lucy's face – Borowczyk simply refuses to cover scenes in the usual manner: there's a master shot, and that shot is of a woman's naked ass! So no cutaways! No reaction shots!). Only in a Borowczyk film does a character masturbate over photos of horses fucking! As before, she's interrupted in her erotic reverie by calls from outside her room.

When the 1975 film cuts back to Lucy again, she's trying on a filmy white dress and veil, as if playing at being a bride. Walerian Borowczyk begins this sequence in a classic manner – with a giant close-up of Lucy's cooch and ass. In an erotic reverie, Lucy admires her naked body under the cloth in the mirror (a classic Borowczykian scene of female autoeroticism).

La Bête finally enters the famous sequence of the monster and the woman, Romilda: it's framed as Lucy's dream or memory or fantasy: she is lying back on her bed, in her gauzy white gown, holding the red rose. The past, two hundred years earlier, is a cultural world of Domenico Scarlatti music – Romilda is first seen playing it in the chateau on a sunny Summer's day (every time *The Beast* cuts back to the forest sequence, the Scarlatti music is pounding away. Why does the harpsichord sound so much heavier than the regular grand piano? The music begins as kind of diegetic, but it continues throughout the sequence, long after Romilda has abandoned the harpsichord in the villa for a romp in the woodland).

Even this intro in *La Bête* is slightly skewed in Walerian Borowczyk's imagination: the establishing shot of Romilda in the chateau is a slow zoom from far off, revealing Romilda in a window. So far so good, but the camera zooms first onto a carving of the god Pan grinning lasciviously (or it could be Dionysius). In other words, primal, mythical desire (an ancient world, a Greek mystery). *Then* it tilts down to reveal Romilda (she's in her early twenties, pretty, white blonde (wearing a wig), refined, small, and alone). Note too that not only is Romilda alone – no servants, butlers, parents, relatives, friends, or visitors insight, she also has no dialogue (but she does scream and cry out a lot!).

There's more mythology evoked before Romilda encounters the beast: Romilda notices that a lamb has wandered away from its mother. No need to point out the symbolism of sacrificial lambs (but also Romilda's maternal instincts). So Romilda goes off in pursuit of the lamb, in a beautiful blue gown and the customary voluminous white under-garments (you can see that actress Sirpa Lane has real trouble running through the overgrown fields and woods in that costume. She must've cursed Borowczyk. Bloody film directors! You come over here and run in this fucking costume!).

The first time that Romilda sees the beast is when she finds the bloody remains of the lamb on the ground, and the beast is nearby. The sight of the corpse and the blood trigger off the hysterical section of this mad version of *Little Red Riding Hood* meets *Beauty and the Beast* meets arty Euro-erotica.

The sex with the beast takes many forms, as if Walerian Borowczyk and his team were riffling through the highlights of the *Kama Sutra*. First, the beast, seen only partially for much of the first fantasies, pursues the woman through the forest. As he chases her, he pulls off pieces of her clothing, a classic sexual fantasy (cut to shots of the clothes flying through the air, catching on bushes, and the monster's point-of-view of Lucy running away from him up a path, the camera focussing on her jiggling cheeks).[22]

By now Romilda is down to a beautiful white corset and socks (piece by piece the costume put together by Piet Bolscher is ripped off). The beast takes up the clothes and sniffs them, and drapes them over his penis (at the

22 The rapidity of the cutting and the density of the images is like a chase in an action movie – a zillion details fly by the viewer.

end of the first chase and rape, in one extraordinary close-up, the beast pulls off her blonde wig and rubs it over the end of his penis, the semen dripping from the hair. There is a dissolve from that close-up of dripping gunk to a close-up of Lucy asleep – Borowczyk is a master of wild juxtapositions).

This's pretty wild stuff. It's so ridiculous, so over-the-top, yet utterly compelling, and it all takes place to the hammering of harpsichord music. Your average sex scene this certainly isn't. Oh yeah, it is a guy in a very silly and unconvincing monster suit chasing a woman in a sunny forest. It's so dumb you can't believe it. It looks like a dumb-ass student movie. And the roars that the sound team (Michel Laurent and Jean-Pierre Ruh) employ for the monster are taken from some Godzilla or dinosaur movie, and don't fit at all.

But all that is deliberate. It's meant to be dumb and unbelievable. As Walerian Borowczyk says, *The Beast* is more a comedy than an erotic film. Maybe. But wait. This isn't just a dumb-ass movie: no silly film would include in the midst of a sex scene sudden cuts to the trees, to a lake, to a snail crawling on a shoe (*no one* cuts away to shots of trees and leaves in the midst of a sex scene or a rape). Something else is going on here.

Romilda takes refuge from the priapic beast in, of all places, a tree (!). While the beast prowls below, brandishing his erection like a club,[23] Romilda falls from the tree, but manages to hold herself up on a branch. Their first sexual coupling is, typically for Walerian

23 Reminiscent of the ithyphallic Cerne Giant chalk hill figure in Dorset, U.K.

Borowczyk, eccentric, to say the least: while she's hanging from a branch, clad only in a white corset and socks, the beast grabs her, burying his muzzle between her legs, eating her pussy. Her feet, meanwhile, as repeated close-ups reveal, touch his phallus. At first she seems to be kicking it or treading on it; then she loses a shoe, aided by the beast (another example of Borowczyk's amazing eye for detail), and masturbates his cock to yet another climax with her feet.

Romilda's screaming and yelling all the way through, and the beast occasionally roars – but Romilda seems to realize that it might be a good idea to get the beast off, and uses her feet to do so. It truly is out-there, off the chain, leftfield, outside the box, whatever: it's one of the weirder sex scenes in cinema: a monster eating a woman's cunt as she hangs from a tree masturbating his cock with her feet, and screaming all the time, while Domenico Scarlatti harpsichord music batters away at the eardrums.

Walerian Borowczyk has challenged the audience: *you want weird? I'll give you weird!*

Meanwhile, back inside the chateau, everyone is asleep – it's *Sleeping Beauty* time, with the people under a spell. Maybe they are all dreaming of Romilda in the forest. A group dream. As if the brutality of the encounter with the beast isn't enough, the violence erupts in the modern-day chateau scenes, as the marquis wakes, hears his uncle pleading with his brother the cardinal not to come to the chateau, and secretly murders his disabled uncle with a razor (covered with anxious point-of-view shots, into the camera). There'a a final, pathetic glimpse of the upturned wheelchair, with blood on its wheels.

Lucy writhes on the bed in her erotic dream, scissoring her legs, pulling her gauzy nightgown back and forth between her thighs. Once again, Walerian Borowczyk & co. hold on this scene far, far longer than dramatically necessary (and also shoots it frontally, from the end of the bed). Three times (three is the key number in fairy tales, of course), Lucy visits Marthurin in his little room nearby, but he remains resolutely asleep (the first time, she goes in and takes off his shoes, presumably to help him sleep better – he tosses about from time to time, as if in fitful dreams. The second time she visits him (wearing the fur coat), she crouches down and puts her hand over his crotch. Like Sleeping Beauty, Mathurin still doesn't wake). There are shots of Lucy's naked body underneath the semi-transparent gown, creeping along the corridors at night, one of Borowczyk's signature images. Borowczyk cuts between Lucy masturbating and fantasizing on her bed and her erotic, 18th century dreams.

This is one horny girl: getting no joy out of Mathurin, she returns to her bedroom and starts to caress the bed knob like it's a dick. Then she washes herself in the bathroom, takes up the red rose (which the marquis gave her with his faked letter from Mathurin), and lies on her bed (one of the recurring motifs in Boro's cinema is that in a state of heightened erotic awarenessm *anything* can become part of the erotic impulse – a flower, a wooden knob, a picture, torn clothing. Boro's cinema genuinely eroticizes the entire world).

One of the longest masturbation scenes in Walerian Borowczyk's cinema ensues (he is certainly one of the kings of the cinema of self-pleasuring – I can't think of another major filmmaker who loves masturbation scenes so much), as Lucy lies back, opens her legs and starts touching herself. An incredible, big close-up: Lucy's cunt, her thighs undulating on either side, her hands covering her sex and she rubs the red rose petals into her labia and clitoris. The shot goes on and on, the red and green of the flower enveloping the woman's vulva, and shielding it from the viewer, her fingers wet, her hands moving back and forth (and it's all in near total silence). The shot ends with Lucy's hands moving out of shot, revealing a close-up of her lips and clit. Wow! *The Beast* then cuts to the final scenes of the woman and the beast. Masturbation – dreaming – creativity – making art. All of life is a fantasy.

The last of the sex scenes between Romilda de l'Esperance and la bête in the woodland occur straight after the remarkable extreme close-up of Lucy masturbating with a red rose. The beast grapples the woman onto a tree trunk and begins to fuck her from behind. Close-ups of his penis, his balls, her buttocks, her face (the editing becomes rapid and fragmentary). Romilda seems to swoon away from the intensity of the experience. Then she comes back to consciousness (expressed with a close-up of her hand, resting on top of her white dress, which begins to move with the rhythm of the beast's movements), and she starts to enjoy what's happening (her gasps are loud, and she licks her lips lasciviously – a classic Borowczyian touch).

The tempo of the cutting increases, as the love-making reaches a climax, which occurs with a money shot, a close-up of the beast coming over the woman's ass (one of many orgasms the beast has). The film then ascends to a plateau of orgasmic pleasures, as the woman and the beast are seen enjoying a variety of sexual acts (Romilda isn't running away now): Romilda squeezing her breasts and nipples to tantalize the beast... the beast fucking her tits... copious amounts of sperm dripping over her body, down to her vulva... Romilda putting her fingers inside herself from behind... Romilda licking the beast's cock as she straddles him... Romilda jerking him with her feet, and so on.

It's Boro's version of the *Kama Sutra*, or Agostino Carracci's *I Modi* (*The Ways*), as Romilda uses her mouth, hands, feet, breasts, hair, ass, vulva and anything else she can think of to get the beast off.

Down on the ground, Romilda masturbates la bête, and licks him again, and he dies (there's blood around his muzzle). There's a final roar, and the Scarlatti music falls away. It's an ecstasy (the 'death's ecstasy' of one of the film's many alternative titles). And that, of course, is one of the recurring fantasies of Western literature. And it's very Surrealist and Sadeian, too: dying at orgasm.

During the sex scenes with the beast, Walerian Borowczyk and his team don't just concentrate on genitals contacting each other, or to close-ups of parts of the eroticized body, as in conventional pornography, he cuts away, many times, to images of the trees and bushes, to a white cloth with blood on it, and to the progress of a snail crawling over Romilda's shoe (the snail, one of many creatures in *La Bête*, is obviously a symbol of phallic fecundity: the snail and shoe features prominently when the beast is fucking Romilda from behind – she stares at it. A phallic snail, a vaginal shoe. The snail and shoe fall to the ground symbolically, just as the beast dies in a series of rapid cuts). *The Beast* also employs subjective shots of Romilda's views of the forest as she's being schtupped: the forest floor, the trees above, with the camera swinging back and forth to simulate the rhythms of sex (Ken Russell used the same technique in *Women In Love* and *Valentino*).

Is it rape? As far as Romilda is concerned, and as far as Lucy fantasizing about the past is concerned, it is rape. But it's a rape they're fantasizing about. Pro-pornography and anti-censorship critics and feminists might say that *The Beast* is extreme, but it does articulate fantasies that some people have (it's not only women who sometimes fantasize about sex with animals). Anti-pornography and pro-censorship critics and feminists might get outraged at that suggestion, and campaign for banning *The Beast* and all of Walerian Borowczyk's films. For them *The Beast* would be a rape fantasy perpetrated by a lecherous film director and pornographer.

For the beast, though, it plainly isn't rape: he just wants to have sex with the woman. Walerian Borowczyk is clear about that: the opening scene of *The Beast* shows animals having sex. It's one of the things they do; get used to it. Issues like neurosis, sexual repression, religion, taboo and the like are human constructs, having *nothing* to do with the animal world. So the beast is like the horse (even his penis looks the same as the horse's). And Borowczyk has explained in interviews that *La Bête* is about the fantasy of having sex with an animal. The *fantasy.*[24] As Borowczyk put it, he is revealing what people dream about. Of course – that's what art does. (I'd say that other rape scenes are far more disturbing than the one in *The Beast*: *The Accused, Deliverance, Straw Dogs,* etc).

⚜

Walerian Borowczyk deploys archetypal tropes in *La Bête*: a lamb, a forest, blood, a chase, a man-beast, a woman alone. The motifs and narratives derive from mythology and fairy tales. What is *La Bête* really, but a European art movie version of *Beauty and the Beast*? It's *Beauty and the Beast* (with a little of *Bluebeard* and *Little Red Riding Hood*), with 1970s eroticism prominent. 'Beauty' and the 'beast' don't dally with each other in restrained conversation, as in the 1945 French version of the fairy tale: they get down to some serious fucking.[25]

La Belle et la Bête is a famous story in French literary history, of course. The most famous fairy tale version was by Mme. Leprince de Beaumont of 1756[26] – altho' Charles Perrault is better known among French authors (along with the Grimm brothers and Hans Christian Andersen, Perrault is one of the founding

---

24 The *fantasy* aspect is utterly crucial: there is nothing remotely 'realistic' about *any* part of *La Bête*.

25 *The Beast* also draws on vampire stories, such as *Carmilla* by Sheridan Le Fanu.

26 The 18th century versions by Madame Leprince de Beaumont (1756, in *Magasin des Enfants*) and Madame Gabrielle de Villeneuve (*Les Contes marin*, 1740) pre-dated that of Charles Perrault (in his *Riquet a la Houppe*, 1697). Mme. d'Aulnoy also published *Beauty and the Beast*-type tales (in *The Ram, The Beneficent Frog* and *The Green Serpent*).

fathers of fairy tale literature). Walerian Borowczyk's film of course draws on the de Beaumont story. The beast and bride or bridegroom story goes back a long way – to Apuleius (*The Golden Ass*, 2nd century), and the myth of Cupid and Psyche, for instance. The story of a woman and an enchanted or supernatural animal is found in many, many places.[27] There are men-pigs in 'Re Porco' by Straparola (mid-16th century), four *Beauty and the Beast* tales in *Pentamerone* by Giambattista Basile (1634-36), and the ancient tale *The Girl Who Married a Snake* (a *Panchatantra* story). Although *The Beast* is a crazee Euro-art movie, it also displays a deep and subtle understanding of folklore and fairy tales.

Beast/ bridegroom tales evoke simple oppositions: beauty and ugliness, female beauty and male ugliness; they have been interpreted as 'finding a mate' stories (by Jack Zipes), as a way of depicting female destiny, of coming to terms with the sexual elements of love, and of harnessing female eroticism.[28]

All beast/ bridegroom tales revolve around selecting a mate and mating rituals, according to Jack Zipes in *The Enchanted Screen*:

> they all represent metaphorically the manner in which young women have been selected for mating. That is, the tales for a large, rich and varied discourse about the selection of makes and how choice is played out to favor them ale bridegrooms. (2011,

27 In folklore studies, *Beauty and the Beast* is a type ATU 425 tale, known as 'The Search For the Lost Husband'. This folk tale type includes 'The Vanished Husband', 'The Animal as Bridegroom', 'The Son of the Witch', 'Beauty and the Beast', 'The Enchanted Husband Sings a Lullaby', 'The Snake as Bridegroom' and 'The Insulted Bridegroom Disenchanted'.
28 See J. Zipes, 2000, 47.

225-6)

But Jack Zipes also notes that despite how much mating rituals and marriage have changed in recent times (and how they vary from culture to culture), movies based on *Beauty and the Beast* and *The Frog Prince* are still conservative and patriarchal, and they still contain 'strong remnants of antiquated views regarding gender roles and the demands placed on women to make sacrifices for daddy and beast' (226).

The most famous film version of *Beauty and the Beast* is the 1945 black-and-white fantasy movie directed by Jean Cocteau, starring Jean Marais. *La Belle et la Bête* has been influential in cinema, not least in the realm of the European art movie, and Walerian Borowczyk also draws on it. More recently, the Walt Disney Company produced a Broadway musical-style interpretation (1991), which drew on Cocteau as well as Mme. Leprince de Beaumont's original tale, and added plenty of Disney touches (such as the animated side-kicks and secondary characters – teapots, candlesticks, clocks). There are many other versions of *Beauty and the Beast* in cinema: Jack Zipes notes 8 silent movies, from 1899-1924, and 29 sound movies, from 1934-2007, in his stupendous book on fairy tale films, *The Enchanted Screen* (see appendix).

In Walerian Borowczyk's and Anatole Dauman's film, though, there is no magical transformation of the beast into the prince. Nope. Instead, Romilda kills the beast, and Lucy appears to kill Mathurin, the modern-day beast (or he dies). No happy ending, then. The ending of

La Bête is fairly ambiguous: Lucy exits in hysteria and remorse, devastated to think she might have killed her bridegroom (whom she liked). And Romilda rushes off along a forest path, now nude (her corset was flung into the lake), and looking distraught (however, she does bury the beast – in a pile of leaves, next to the pillar).

None of the well-known versions of *Beauty and the Beast* come anywhere near the outrage and wildness of Walerian Borowczyk's 1975 film. There have been other modern interpretations in literature – feminists have tackled fairy tales, writing their own (sometimes eroticized) versions. (For the best introduction to fairy tales, go to the writings of Jack Zipes).[29]

The Beast also draws on aspects of *Little Red Riding Hood*: the young woman in the forest and the wolf (some modern fairy tales have eroticized the encounter between the young woman and the wolf). You don't have to know anything about Sigmund Freud or Bruno Bettelheim or Jack Zipes to see what's going on in *Little Red Riding Hood*. In a way, *The Beast* is *Little Red Riding Hood* in the forest (and in the past), and *Beauty and the Beast* inside the chateau (and the present day).

There is also a little of *Bluebeard* – Walerian Borowczyk loves the trope of the forbidden room or the tabooed cabinet, and uses it in other films. In *Immoral*

29 Jack Zipes is one of the very best contemporary commentators on fairy tales, on a par with any of the celebrated critics, such as Bruno Bettelheim, Marie-Louise van Franz or the Grimms themselves. If you want an excellent introduction to fairy tales, you can't do better than reading Jack Zipes.
All of Jack Zipes's books are truly wonderful, but some of the best are *Don't Bet on the Prince*, 1983, *The Oxford Companion To Fairy Tales*, 2000, *Breaking the Spell*, 2002, and *Sticks and Stones*, 2002. See bibliography.

Tales, the ultimate *Bluebeard* story is enacted by the Countess Bathóry who has virgins slaughtered for their blood.

The red rose in *The Beast*, one of the talismanic objects of the film (including Walt Disney's version), also comes straight out of fairy tales, including *Beauty and the Beast*. But fairy tale heroines like Belle or Snow White would never dream of using a rose to rub over their clitorises.

In *The Beast*, a young woman enters a forest: the forest is typically the place in fairy tales where characters enter in order to encounter obstacles and mystery. The forest is the place of initiation and trial. It lies on the edge of the familiar, everyday world of the fairy tale. It is where the protagonist gets lost, meets strange creatures, undergoes transformations and spells. It is, typically, one of the first places the protagonist enters on the journey outwards from the home, in *Snow White, Little Red Riding Hood* or *Hansel and Gretel*, for example.

In *The Brothers Grimm*, Jack Zipes writes of the forest in fairy tales:

> Inevitably, they find their way into the forest. It is there that they lose and find themselves. It is there that they gain a sense of what is to be done. The forest is always large, immense, great, and mysterious. No one ever gains power of the forest, but the trees possess the power to change lives and alter destinies. (43)

The forest is a zone of otherness, strangeness, enchantment and the unknown. In (Jungian) psychological terms, it is the unconscious, or confusion, a realm of instability, a *regressus ad uterum*, a place of recreation and rebirth, where the ego/ soul/ hero/ine is tested and initiated. The enchanted or dark forest is a place of wild things, such as dragons in caves, or witches in their gloomy houses; it is also a place of death (and dragons, witches, caves and darkness are linked with death or the 'dark side' of life). *The Beast* evokes many of those aspects, with love and death foremost.

As Jack Zipes notes, no one controls the dark forest, though it may control you. It represents something wilder, stranger, darker and more mysterious than any individual; the natural world, a plenitude that can be life-giving as well as threatening or death-dealing.

The dark forest also has a 'feminine'/ uterine/ womb association, for it is the place of rebirth. The places in fairy tales linked with the dark forest (caves, marshes, deserts, wells, seas, underworlds) are also 'feminine'/ birth spaces. Entering the dark forest is essentially the 'descent and return' process of mythology (Orpheus, Jesus, Theseus, Persephone, Isis and others descended into the Underworld or Hell and returned changed and/ or reborn). The descent is towards the foundation of life, to the secret heart of nature. The initiate (whether Orpheus, Hansel, Little Red Riding Hood or Persephone) has to overcome fear and doubt, and learn courage and resourcefulness. Often a monster has to be encountered and sometimes slain (Theseus and the Minotaur, Perseus and St George against the dragon, Marduk and the monster Tiamat, Zeus and the Titans, or Jack and the giant).

Walerian Borowczyk takes up mythic material – a woman and a monster – which's the basic stuff of countless horror films. And it's filmed like a horror movie, too – with blurry, handheld shots, the camera operator (Gérard Wurtz) running behind or in front of the actors, with the woman's screams prominent. Like horror pictures, the viewer sees glimpses of parts of the bodies, and only fragments of the beast (only towards the end are full shots of the beast included). And yet, no horror film I've seen would think of putting (or dare to put) Domenico Scarlatti harpsichord music over a monster chasing a woman. The music is simply *unbelievable*. I bet that Scarlatti has *never* been used over a monster chase in a movie.[30]

In horror films, one of the things the monster threatens to do is to fuck the heroine. Well, Walerian Borowczyk simply makes good that threat, and the monster really does fuck the heroine. In horror cinema, the question is, will he catch her?, and what will he do to her if he does? In American horror movies, the monster's going to kill her, or torture her, but Borowczyk's *La Bête* makes it all very clear: no, he doesn't want to cut her up like your typical slasher villain, he wants to fuck her. In this respect, again, *La Bête* is not pornographic: rather, it's all those stalk 'n' slash and serial killer movies that are really pornographic, with their truly twisted emphasis on violence and endless suffering.

One of the central motifs of *La Bête* is the beast's phallus – the spectator sees much more of this than the

30 And you can bet that Scarlatti would never have dreamt his music would be used in *this* manner!

whole of the beast himself. Indeed, one of the first sightings of the beast is of his massive penis. It's permanently erect (nothing's limp in erotica!), dribbles healthy doses of sperm (over the woman's breasts, buttocks, vulva, mouth, hair, feet), and is the target of much licking, stroking and tupping.

The Beast is a movie of many cocks, actually: there's the horse cock at the beginning, in the second shot of the whole movie, and Ifany's large joystick, and drawings of penises that Lucy finds on two occasions. And the beast's schlong of course is shaped like a horse's penis.

The ithyphallic beast is the incarnation of wild, unbridled sexuality, restlessly, endlessly priapic, a totally stereotypical embodiment of male sexual lust, with an unstoppable carnal drive. He is the epitome of lusty satyrs and Pans out of Greek mythology, the wolves, bears and ogres of fairy tales, the monsters of legend and horror films. Walerian Borowczyk gives the beast (and the design of its phallus) a clear origin in the horses that Lucy stumbles upon copulating in the stables at the beginning of the film. (The beast itself resembles, apart from a man in a hairy suit, a wolf and a bear).

HYSTERIA IN *THE BEAST*.

The hysteria of both Lucy and Romilda in *The Beast* chimes with the hysteria of the virgins in *Immoral Tales*, the nuns in *Behind Convent Walls,* and the violence of Miriam Gwen in *Love Rites*: women on the edge is something that fascinates Walerian Borowczyk. It's worth noting that there is a huge amount of theoretical writing about the links between insanity, hysteria and altered states of consciousness and the relation to religion. Contemporary feminism, for instance, has studied mediaeval religious hysteria, which relates directly to Boro's cinema.

Instead of using the usual approach of Sigmund Freud, the writings of French feminism are useful in thinking about the depiction of the women in *The Beast*, or the nuns and the religious communities in *Behind Convent Walls*. Luce Irigaray, for instance, has been concerned with the notion of women as 'outsiders', of the otherness and outsideness of women in a patriarchal regime. Irigaray is interested in those women who have been 'outsiders' in history – the hysteric, the witch, the mediæval mystic, those people who 'stand outside' culture, using the techniques of ecstasy ('ex-stase', Irigaray spells it, 'ecstasy' meaning, from the Greek, 'stand outside'). Both Irigaray and Julia Kristeva spoke of the special creative positionality of the mediæval women mystics, who occupied the maternal liminal place of the mother, where the object of devotion became less fixed, more open, less dogmatic, more 'feminine'.

For Julia Kristeva (in *Tales of Love*), Christianity offers a limited number of ways in which women can participate in the 'symbolic Christian order': for women who are not virgins or nuns, who have orgasms and give birth

> her only means of gaining access to the symbolic paternal order is by engaging in an endless struggle between the orgasmic maternal body and the symbolic prohibition – a struggle that will take the form of guilt and mortification, and culminate in

> masochistic *jouissance*. For a woman who has not easily repressed her relationship with her mother, participation in the symbolic paternal order as Christianity defines it can only be masochistic.[31]

Two of the classic ways in which women have been allowed to participate in Christianity is the '*ecstatic* and the *melancholy*' (ib.). According to Elizabeth Grosz in "Lesbian Fetishism?", women can disavow their own castration (*contra* Sigmund Freud) through hysteria – women phallicizing part of their bodies; the 'masculine complex' – women taking the phallus as their love object; and narcissism – women turning their bodies into the phallus.[32] This theoretical discussion bears directly on *The Beast*.

THE APOCALYPTIC ENDING.

The revelation, in the final scenes, that Mathurin is really the beast, is a hackneyed but effective way of connecting the fantasy and 'real life' narratives, the past and the present. Mathurin is found dead beside his bed by Lucy, on her third and final visit to her future husband; she becomes hysterical, and Walerian Borowczyk has Lisbeth Hummel play the subsequent scenes at the height of hysteria. The madness comes from Lucy thinking she has killed Mathurin, just as Romilda killed the beast in her fantasy and in the past ('I didn't do anything!' Lucy repeatedly tells her aunt Virginia). Lucy thinks she has killed him in her erotic fantasies: in her dreams, as Romilda literally fucks the beast to death,

31 J. Kristeva, *Tales of Love*, tr. L.S. Roudiez, Columbia University Press, New York, 1987, 147.
32 E. Grosz, "Lesbian fetishism?", *Differences*, 3, 2, 1991.

using all her charms until the beast lies down and dies (both beasts die at the same time).

It's as if women, once sexually aroused, have too much desire, too much orgasmic pleasure, for the men or beasts to sustain. It's as if female erotic desire overwhelms the men, in the end, and kills them. Although the beast has multiple orgasms and is the embodiment of pure sexual lust, in the end it's Romilda's sexual desire that kills him. And notice how Lucy arrives at the chateau in a state of sexual excitement: she's leaping out of the car and photographing the forest; she's searching around her room and finding erotic illustrations; and she's masturbating a number of times. Once aroused, her erotic desire becomes unstoppable (though not necessarily insatiable – she just wants a man to love, and is eager to get on with her marriage. Note that in the dinner scene, Virginia is repulsed by Mathurin suddenly talking about tobacco and chewing it, but Lucy is more forgiving. And it's Virginia who undresses Mathurin at the end to reveal him as the beast).

It's noteworthy, too, that it's *Lucy* who pursues *Mathurin*, not the other way around. Mathurin is actually scared, he tells his father, and would prefer not to be presented for marriage. Mathurin is weak, vulnerable, withdrawn, and not at all beast-like – which makes perfect dramatic sense.[33] In the forest/ past sequence, it's the beast who pursues Romilda (although Romilda does go into the forest willingly, to catch the

33 However, he is pretty simple and uncouth: in the dinner scene, he descends into a paroxysm of imbecility when his father berates him for stuffing tobacco into his maw when they're supposed to be having a civilized dinner.

lamb). In the chateau/ present-day sequence, it's the woman pursing the man; she is the modern woman, predatory, making all the first moves. But both beasts die.

Notice, too, that Lucy never stops wanting and loving Mathurin: despite his appearance, despite countless signals, and despite her aunt's misgivings,[34] Lucy holds fast to her love for this uncouth, unappealing guy (one of the aspects of *The Beast* that stretches credibility is that Lucy and Mathurian have been corresponding b4 meeting. No way would Mathurin be able to string to two words together; once again, it has to be the scheming marquis).

In the scenes which close *The Beast*, Walerian Borowczyk employs negative space: characters move out of frame for some moments, although they can be heard talking. Mathurin is picked up by the others, woken by a hysterical Lucy banging on the doors; he's put into a chair in the hall, then taken into the living room, where's he's laid on a table (on a red rug).

It's Virginia who undresses Mathurin, revealing a very hairy body and a tail. It's a grotesque image of a man-beast (actually quite creepy, and more effective than the beast costume). At that point, the reaction of Virginia is to get out of there as quickly as possible, taking Lucy with her (Lucy eventually calms down when she's in the Roller).

34 Notice too that there are no scenes of Lucy and Mathurin alone together: the only time is when Mathurin is asleep and Lucy creeps into his room. Apart from that, they are always in social situations, surrounded by people. It's as if the movie doesn't want to explore just what Lucy and Mathurin would do together – so it never gives them the chance (of course, being about to wed, there is also that social prohibition).

What the discovery of Mathurin as the beast does is to unleash a vitriolic denunciation of bestiality by the Cardinal, who has finally arrived (he encounters Virginia and the half-naked Lucy leaving). The Cardinal's detestation of bestial sex is absurdly graphic (he talks about women who use dogs and cats to lick their vulvas).[35]

The ending of *The Beast* has an apocalyptic air to it: it's Lucy's sobbing hysteria that induces the unreality and intensity. Altho' *The Beast* is no tragic play like *Othello* or *Oedipus Rex*, it does climax with a series of deaths: the marquis kills his uncle de Balo, the two beasts die, and in his final appearance, on the roof of the chateau, the marquis flourishes his razor, suggesting that he might be going to kill himself.

At the end of *The Beast,* the filmmakers have Lucy play the final scenes naked: Lucy's nudity has a primal, mythical element to it, a return not to a Garden of Eden, pre-Fall innocence, but a savage, primal knowledge. As if, encountering death for the first time, face-to-face, Lucy reverts to a primitive state (it's a move from innocence to hysteria, bypassing knowledge). No coincidence, either, that the filmmakers have Lucy put on the fur coat: it's as if she has become the beast herself.

There's plenty of religious subtext to *The Beast*, too, as in all of Walerian Borowczyk's work. At the top layer, the Duc De Balo, is constantly telephoning the Vatican to speak to the Cardinal whom they hope will come and marry Mathurin to Lucy. The marriage, like the baptism,

35 In *The Beast,* Walerian Borowczyk and his team stage scenes where half-naked or completely naked characters (usually women), in states of desire or madness or dislocation, face people (usually authority figures) who are fully dressed.

will they hope nix the curse of the beast (Mathurin isn't baptized, but the marquis soon fixes that).

Deeper layers of religiosity in *The Beast* include the familiar oppositions of paganism vs. religion, nature vs. civilization (the forest vs. the chateau), 'normal sex' (Clarisse and Ifany) and bestial sex (Romilda and the beast). The Cardinal condemns bestiality, yet this wilfully over-the-top movie has Romilda being raped by an animal but then enjoying it, and going further than the beast himself in sex, and fucking him to death.

The blasphemy of the 1975 movie is to reveal a morality that Christianity and civilized society would prefer to repress or ignore: that humans have lusts and appetites that can be as unbridled as that of animals. Animals fuck – it's one of the things they do (the horses are seen coupling at the beginning of *The Beast*), and some humans love to fuck, too (if they didn't, we wouldn't be here). The film depicts lustful characters: Lucy, Clarisse, Ifany, the beast, Romilda – even the curé has his pretty boys (which he creepily fondles and kisses).[36]

The Beast is thus an attack on the hypocrisies of organized religion (and Catholicism in particular). It makes it clear that the people who run religion are themselves degenerate (*viz.*, the priest with his under-age boys).

⚜

36 The choirboys are played by Thierry Bourdon (Modeste), and a girl, Anna Baldaccini (Théodore). Maybe the filmmakers thought it's not so shocking if the actor playing the curé (Roland Armontel) is groping a girl.

JOUISSANCE IN FRENCH FEMINISM.

Second wave feminists of the Andrea Dworkin, Catherine Mackinnon, Susan Griffin and Susan Brownmiller kind (that is, Anglo-American second feminists), would no doubt denounce *The Beast* as sexist, macho crap, just as they denounced *Deep Throat, Emmanuelle* and other 1970s porn movies. Yet there is in *The Beast* a depiction of unbridled female sexuality – embodied in Lucy Broadhurst in the present and Romilda in the past, which is so powerful it overwhelms the beasts in their lives.

When feminists discuss the body and sexuality, the results are just as controversial as their discussions of issues such as art vs. pornography, or the ways in which female power can be asserted in the social and political arena. However, many feminists, in particular French feminists of the 1970s and 1980s, speak of the sexual superiority of women, or, if not 'superiority', then at least a sexuality that is more sophisticated, more dangerous, more exhilarating, more subtle, and more sensual – well, that amounts to 'superior'. For instance, Xavière Gauthier, a contemporary of the trio of French feminists and philosophers, Hélène Cixous, Luce Irigaray and Julia Kristeva, says that:

> ...witches [women] are bursting; their entire bodies are desire; their gestures are caresses; their smell, taste, hearing are all sensual. Their pleasure is so violent, so transgressive, so open, so fatal, that men have not yet recovered... Female eroticism is terrifying; it is an earthquake, a volcanic eruption, a tidal wave. It is disquieting and so is mystified. It is

made a mystery.[37]

This transgressive, terrifying eroticism has not yet really been depicted in art or pornography for feminists. What one gets is men's version of it – male ideas of wild eroticism, with violence as a recurring ingredient. Hélène Cixous reckons that women have an 'infinite', 'cosmic' libido, an eroticism which is always in flux, and so minute and subtle, it goes far beyond male/ masculine sexuality.

> Almost everything is yet to be written by women about femininity: about their sexuality, that is, its infinite and mobile complexity, about their eroticization, sudden turn-ons of a certain miniscule-immense area of their bodies; not about destiny, but about the adventure of such and such a drive, about trips, crossings, trudges, abrupt and gradual awakenings, discoveries of a zone at one time timorous and soon to be forthright. A woman's body, with its thousand and one thresholds of ardor...[38]

Women have an all-over, total body eroticism, say writers such as Anaïs Nin, Peter Redgrove and Luce Irigaray (and so do some men!). 'But *woman has sex organs just about everywhere*. She experiences pleasure almost everywhere', asserts Luce Irigaray (yes, but so do many men!).[39] Feminists have spoken of the wildness of women's eroticism and their fantasies (which's precisely

37 Xavière Gauthier, in Elaine Marks, 1981, 201-2.
38 In E. Marks, 256.
39 L. Irigaray: "Ce sexe qui n'en est pas un", in E., Marks, 103; see also: Jane Gallop, *Feminism and Psychoanalysis: The Daughter's Seduction*, Macmillan, 1983, 77-83; Elizabeth Grosz: "Philosophy, subjectivity and the body", in Carole Pateman & Elizabeth Grosz, eds. *Feminist Challenges*, Allen & Unwin, Sydney, 1986, 125-43.

what *The Beast* explores – let's not forget that the two main protagonists in both past and present are women). What this stance does is to uphold the eternal philosophical dualism of the West, setting women always against men, and using men to gauge women's sexuality. Feminists such as Hélène Cixous have argued, rightly, that masculine 'binary logic', which constantly opposes terms such as 'masculine' and 'feminine', is very limiting. It is two-term logocentrism, which reduces everything to 'yes' or 'no'.[40]

Luce Irigaray in her famous description of women's sexuality says women have an all-over eroticism, a total body sensuality, where the whole of the skin is alive to touches. 'The whole of my body is sexuate. My sexuality isn't restricted to my sex and to the sexual act (in the narrow sense)', writes Irigaray.[41] For Irigaray, a woman's sex is 'two lips which embrace continually', in which women are parthenogenic, and self-contained, not needing others to pleasure them, because 'they are pleasuring themselves – continually'.

Nancy Friday has collected women's fantasies in a number of books: *My Secret Garden, Women On Top* and *Forbidden Flowers*.[42] The fantasies involve lesbianism, group sex, sex with animals, sex with pop and movie stars, rape, anal sex, domination, S/M and all manner of erotic activities (many of which Walerian Borowczyk has explored in his cinema). Women's

40 H. Cixous, *The Newly Born Woman*, tr. Betsy Wing, Minnesota University Press, Minneapolis, 1986, 63f.
41 L. Irigaray, *Je, tu, nous: Toward a Culture of Difference*, tr. Alison Martin, Routledge, 1993, 53.
42 Nancy Friday: *Forbidden Flowers: More Women's Sexual Fantasies*, Arrow, 1993.

fantasies, like their fictions, are, some feminists believe, wilder, larger, more amazing and more frightening, to use Susan Griffin's words, than male fantasies and fictions.[43]

Luce Irigaray talks about the 'very openness' of women's bodies, 'of their flesh, of their genitals', so that boundaries become difficult to define.[44] Irigaray speaks of two kinds of erotic *jouissance* – the phallic kind of orgasm, which men are concerned with and brag about – and the *jouissance* in harmony with a female libidinal economy (ib., 45). Irigaray's point is that there are forms of *jouissance* other than the phallocratic model. Incredible though women's sexual fantasies may be, they are always defined in terms of male fantasies, often in terms of difference.

THE BEAST AND OTHER WALERIAN BOROWCZYK MOVIES.

Three Immoral Women (a.k.a. *Les Héroïnes du mal, Heroines of Evil, Heroines of Pain* and *Immoral Women,* 1979), has affinities with *The Beast*: it's classic Walerian Borowczyk, truly outrageous: this is a film where a young woman masturbates with her pet rabbit.

The second episode of *Three Immoral Women,* 'Marceline', focusses on Gaëlle Legrand as a young woman in 19th century France, the daughter of

43 See, for instance, Lonnie Barbach, ed. *Pleasures: Women Write Erotica,* Doubleday, New York, 1984; Laura Duesing: *Three West Coast Women,* Five Fingers Poetry, 1987; Clayton Eshleman, ed. *Caterpillar Anthology*, Anchor, 1971; Lynne Tillman: *Weird Fucks,* 1980; Jane Hirshfield: *Of Gravity and Angels,* Wesleyan University Press, 1988; Jayne Anne Phillips: *Black Tickets,* Delacorte Press, 1979; Marilyn Hacker: *Love, Death and the Changing of the Seasons,* Arbor House, 1986.
44 *The Irigaray Reader,* ed. Margaret Whitford, Blackwell, Oxford, 1991, 112.

bourgeois parents. The episode was based on a story by Walerian Borowczyk's regular collaborator André Pieyre de Mandiargues. Again, this episode is a slice of prime Walerian Borowczyk: only Borowczyk would depict an extended scene of a young woman masturbating on a lawn with her pet rabbit.

Certainly the scene where Marceline masturbates with the rabbit between her legs on the lawn in the Summer sun, early on in the episode, is one of the more outrageous chapters in the Walerian Borowczyk cinematic *Book of Erotica*.[45] Framing is everything here, as the film includes a parasol prop which partially obscures Marceline's naked body and the rabbit nibbling at her vulva. The film also selects very low angles throughout the scene, a kind of rabbit's-eye-view of female masturbation, the camera squints along Marceline's nude form from between her legs, to her breasts and face. Borowczyk knows better than anyone that *selective* images of the body or a sex act are classic elements in erotica, which he also employs throughout *The Beast* (but he's not averse to having plenty of wholly nude people in his films too). The movie lingers over Marceline caressing her breasts in close-up at length, erecting her nipples.

The rabbit masturbation scene is truly Out There, and it's made even more peculiar because of Walerian Borowczyk's touches – the clever framing and camera angles, the performance of the actress, the near-silence

45 The 'Marceline' episode opens with the girl dancing on the lawn with the rabbit. One can imagine the auditions for this film: 'what do I have to do, Monsieur Borowczyk?' 'Oh, you have to strip off in a garden in the sun and masturbate with a rabbit.' 'Oh.' 'Yes.' 'OK, *d'accord*, I'll do it!'

(just Marceline's gasps and whispered encouragements to her pet rabbit – *The Beast* also includes a soundtrack of nothing but erotic gasps). And as it's masturbation, of course it has to be interrupted – by the maid calling Marceline to dinner. A huge number of Borowczyk's sex scenes are interrupted – just as they are in erotic art throughout history.

In *Three Immoral Women,* Marceline is raped by the black butcher Petrus. Marceline's sexual curiosity and pleasure is punished twice (there is the race element, too, of course, which also cropped up in films such as *The Beast*, with its negative stereotyping of black men).

In the second episode of *Three Immoral Women,* Marceline takes revenge on her oppressors. She kills her mother, her father, and her rapist, the butcher, Petrus (Hassane Fall, who was the butler Ifany in *The Beast*), hangs himself.

Another scene of bestiality occurs in 1983's *Art of Love.* Perhaps the oddest sex scene in *Ars Amandi* (among many), is Claudia's dream of copulating with a bull in a misty, smoky forest, as she imagines herself as Pasiphæ, Queen of Crete; in this bizarre ritual, surrounded by Roman guards and heralds with trumpets, Claudia climbs (naked, of course) into a wooden replica of a cow, and presents her buttocks through a circular hole at the rear to a man dressed in a giant wooden bull's head and wielding a huge bull's pizzle.

Yes, but it's not that simple: *Art of Love* cuts from Claudia on her bed fantasizing, to Claudia as Pasiphæ inside the bull, to the man fucking her,[46] to Ovid narrating the scene in the lecture hall, and finally to a real bull and cow going at it in a field (in a different setting). Walerian Borowczyk's editing here is extraordinary. Sometimes the montages in Boro's films are so rapid and so deft, you're not quite sure what you've seen. It's so many layers of narration, of dreams within stories.

In the museum the servant Sepora fondles the genitals of a horse, and in Claudia's imagination a woman caresses a real horse's cock, shot from the same low angle (the museum seems to feature plaster reproductions of statues, a common way of displaying sculptures).

⚜

I see I've written quite a bit about *The Beast* – there is a lot to it, once you get beyond the sheer silliness of it all. On a script and narrative level, *The Beast* is actually cleverly worked out (including how the fantasy two hundred years ago impacts on the present day story). And while the monster suit and the chase is pure pantomime or vaudeville, there are some impressive technical effects in *The Beast*, but many of them are invisible: the editing, for a start (courtesy of the maestro and an army of editorial assistants). Nearly always the last thing viewers and critics comment upon in Walerian Borowczyk's cinema (hell, there's all that naked flesh to contemplate first), the editing in Borowczyk's films is virtuosic. It's as impressive as any of Borowczyk's contemporary European art filmmakers. Really? Yes. Oh sure, Jean-Luc

46 There are of course close-ups of the red pizzle entering Claudia.

Godard or Ingmar Bergman are taken so seriously in other areas of filmmaking (politically, psychologically, socially), but at the level of editing and organizing material, Borowczyk is a magician. Just look at the way he's bringing together all of the characters in *The Beast*.

One of the curious aspects of Walerian Borowczyk's montage style of editing is that he leaves in parts of shots most other editors would automatically throw to the cutting room floor: wobbly camerawork, parts of shots where the camera operator is lining up a shot, or the sudden slew of a camera up and down as they finish a tilting move. Borowczyk seems to like those parts of shots before he called 'action!' and after he'd called 'cut!'

The other invisible technical element in *The Beast* is the music. Oh sure, Vincente Minnelli or Martin Scorsese are regularly trotted out as amazing film directors when it comes to music (and they are), but just for the use of the Domenico Scarlatti score alone in *The Beast*, Walerian Borowczyk is the equal of his contemporaries.

And for simply taking the viewer to a place all of its own, a dream-like forest of the unconscious, where desires run rampant, *The Beast* is extraordinary.

Walerian Borowczyk should be celebrated as one of cinema's true originals, a filmmaker with a vision wilfully eccentric, determinedly personal and individual, indulgently lyrical, boundlessly imaginative, and shamelessly erotic. You have to admire someone who said, fuck it, I'm going to do what *I* want, I'm going to create mesmerizing hallucinations, entire worlds. Borowczyk's was a cinema of magical spaces, a surreal city of dreams...

...somewhere on Earth (probably Paris), a partially-clothed and beautiful woman (who looks a lot like Leda) is washing herself in an antique bathtub in a *fin-de-siècle* apartment art-directed to perfection by a Renaissance master to the strains of Handel and Scarlatti.

APPENDICES

QUOTES BY WALERIAN BOROWCZYK

La Bête is a fantasy film and especially an 'adult film'. But first of all it is a film about dream mechanisms. Dreams translate our deepest desires. Why then cover with a veil of silence the temptation of an intimate relationship with an animal?

⚜

All stages of a film's creation are in me at one and the same time. My temperament does not allow me to create only part of a work and then to entrust the rest to specialists... I... eliminate the collaborators who dare to try and barter my own ideas with me. *I know everything.* And that very often drives members of my crew to tears.

⚜

I attach a great deal of importance to details

⚜

I conceive all my films in an instant, and only objective means prevent me from making them in that instant.

⚜

Eroticism, sex, is one of the most moral parts of life. Eroticism does not kill, exterminate, encourage evil, lead to crime. On the contrary, it makes people gentler, brings joy, gives fulfilment, leads to selfless pleasure.

⚜

If I have to choose an epoch and an identity, it

would be that of Leda's swan in antiquity (if she really was as beautiful as the artists represent her).

OTHER VERSIONS OF *BEAUTY AND THE BEAST*

BEAUTY AND THE BEAST: THE WALT DISNEY COMPANY

For Walerian Borowczyk, the movies of the Walt Disney Company were more pornographic than his own pictures! It's an unusual view, but in keeping with Boro's sense of the absurd. For Borowczyk, *Snow White and the Seven Dwarfs* was much more erotic than any of his own films because of its 'stench of unsatisfied desire'. The Walt Disney corporation produced one of the two most well-known versions of *Beauty and the Beast* in 1991 (the one other one is the movie of 1945 produced by André Paulvé and directed by Jean Cocteau).

In fact, like many of Walt Disney's movies, *Beauty and the Beast* seethes with erotic desire, look at the dynamic shifts of scene, the torrent of visual images, the vivid colours, the unspoken desires. But it is all unresolved: the filmmakers have studiously avoided erotic desire, even though they also foreground it.

Beauty and the Beast was a great success for Disney, making $352m worldwide, and selling nearly 22 million videos (*The Little Mermaid* had sold 9 million tapes a year before). And it was rightly nominated for an Oscar. But the title song won an Oscar. Sequels followed, as well as the inevitable TV series. And also a Broadway show (1994, with a book by Linda Woolverton, lyrics by Howard Ashman and Tim Rice, and music by Alan Menken. It opened at the Palace Theatre in Gotham).

Like more recent Disney films such as *The Little Mermaid* and *Pocahontas*, *Beauty and the Beast* had a strong, proto-feminist female character at its centre. In the 1980s and 1990s Disney seemed to be consciously alternating between creating strong heroines (Beauty, Pocahontas, the Mermaid, Mulan), and action-adventure heroes (Hercules, Simba, Quasimodo, Aladdin). The main cinematic reference point for Disney's *Beauty and the Beast* was clearly the classic European art movie *La Belle et La Béte,* directed by the Surrealist French poet Jean Cocteau (as well as the CBS television series of fairy tales of the late 1980s). (However, the Disney animators were advised not to watch Cocteau's classic. Why? Because it has such a distinctive look, and because it's such a compelling film. The French film does crop up in the Disney film at many points. The design of the prince, for instance, evoked Jean Marais).

At first, *Beauty and the Beast* was due to be directed by Richard Purdum and produced by Don Hahn, who had worked on *Who Framed Roger Rabbit?*. The Hahn-Purdum team visited the Loire valley to research the French settings and culture for *Beauty and the Beast*; they produced story reels from their trip, but executive Jeffrey Katzenberg found them too dark. Howard Ashman, lyricist on *The Little Mermaid*, was brought in to develop the film. Purdum resigned from the project, and Kirk Wise and Gary Trousdale, from the story department, were hired to direct. Hahn continued as producer. The producer-director team of Hahn-Wise-Trousdale would become one of the most successful in Disney's history.

Linda Woolverton (b. 1952), the scriptwriter on *Beauty and the Beast*, had worked for CBS, children's theatre, written some novels for teenagers, two animated stories for Disney television, co-wrote *Mulan,* and added to *The Lion King* (she later wrote 2010's *Alice In*

Wonderland). Woolverton researched *Beauty and the Beast* by reading all the versions of the story, and much of the writing surrounding it (but I bet she didn't watch *The Beast*!). She said she was intrigued by a Disney heroine who was studious, cultured, who read books.[1]

The story of *Beauty and the Beast* was developed at the script stage, with Belle, not her father, going to the Beast's castle; Gaston, the proud, vain and bland village bully, became a villain; secondary characters, such as Cogsworth, the majordomo turned into a mantle clock (the fussy British butler stereotype), Mrs Potts, the cook and teapot (the warm-hearted mother figure), Chip, her cup son, and Lumiere, the French waiter and candlestick (the suave, smooth-talking French stereotype), were developed to provide entertainment in the second act, where Belle is in the Beast's castle.

Those characters, like Gaston, were additions to the Mme. Leprince de Beaumont story, as were elements such as Belle's father being an inventor, Gaston's sidekick, xx, the plotting of Gaston to win Belle, Gaston's three sexy admirers, the clever horse, xx. (Mme. Leprince de Beaumont's tale, like most fairy tales, is simply too short for a feature-length movie, although *Beauty and the Beast*, at 84 minutes, is shorter than many recent movies. And all the better for it – contemporary films, not only Hollywood movies, are too often too long).

According to Marina Warner, Linda Woolverton and the scriptwriters on *Beauty and the Beast* must have steeped themselves in the history of the fairy tale, as well as feminist debates. 'This fairy tale film is more vividly aware of contemporary sexual politics than any made before', Warner reckoned in *From the Beast to the Blonde* (313). Warner suggested that Woolverton and the script team had grown up with feminists such as Gloria Steinem and Betty Friedan and had daughters who were

1 B. Thomas, 1991, 143.

into Sinéad O'Connor and Madonna. However, despite this Disney heroine being brave, self-aware, ambitious, it was the Beast who stole the film (M. Warner, 314).

The Beast was huge, pneumatic, looked like a bull, with a mane, horns, claws, fangs, and large shoulders. The Beast was 'male desire incarnate. He embodies the Eros figure as phallic toy. The Beast swells, he towers, he inflates, he tumesces', wrote Marina Warner (1995, 315). Exactly – and that's also the Beast in Walerian Borowczyk's erotic-comic take on the tale! Except that Boro and his team put into their movie the erect phallus, which the Disney movie of course doesn't; instead, in the familiar manner of mainstream cinema, Disney shifts erotic desire and phallic, clitoral energy into synecdoches and correspondences.

The Beast in the 1991 musical movie evokes the Minotaur of ancient myth, and also the American buffalo, the animal associated with the Wild West. The American buffalo connoted back-to-the-land goodness.[2] It's true that when the Beast's on screen, he does dominate the action – partly because of his unpredictability: you don't know what he's going to do next. How dangerous is he, really? He might do anything. His servants, Potts, Lumiere and Cogsworth, are all afraid of him (the animators build in plenty of moments when the servants scatter in fear, then creep back in slowly as the Beast calms down). But Belle is equally watchable, and it's very much her story and her film; on watching the picture again, Belle stands out as the central component in the story – without her, there would still be plenty to enjoy – no doubt the Disney animators and story dept could string out endless episodes between the Beast and

2 Glen Keane, who animated the Beast, looked at many wild animals (wolves, gorillas, mandrills, bears, boars, tigers) before arriving at the final design, which combined the muzzle and beard of the buffalo, the brow of the gorilla, a lion's mane, a boar's tusks, the ibis's hairy neck, a wolf's tail and a bear's body; the horns were added by Keane.

his servants in the castle, for instance. But Belle gives the movie more than 'heart' or 'emotion': she embodies what's at stake, and she drives the narrative (for instance, one of her primary acts has nothing to do with the Beast plot: it is to resist Gaston, who's incredibly forceful in his advances to Belle. Indeed, some of the scenes involving Belle and Gaston are very physical and come close to rape scenarios (again, Borowczyk & co. simply make explicitly what Disney and contemporary American cinema suppresses, by depicting the rape). When Gaston falls to his death at the end, it is largely because he has attempted to kill the Beast – and he succeeds. But Gaston must die also because of his vile treatment of Belle – and her father. One of his bizarre nasty plots, which nearly works, is to have Belle's father carted off to a mental asylum).

From the beginning, Belle is portrayed in *Beauty and the Beast* as a different kind of Disney heroine. She is bookish, for a start: she's another version of the Disney dreamer, and an outsider (*The Beast* makes Lucy Broadhurst a dreamer – that's a vital element of her personality, and of many Borowczykian protagonists, including Goto. Lucy is also surrounded by books and pictures). Belle's books and reading distinguish her from the rest of the village, and in the village's song about her they express their distrust of someone who can read (it might be popular culture's mistrust of eggheads and geeks). *Beauty and the Beast* is thus also about fairy tales and storytelling themselves – a commentary upon them. Belle even reads out part of a story and comments upon it.[3]

Belle's father, meanwhile, is the familiar bumbling but lovable and kindly father (who's also, in typical Disney tradition, an inventor). It's crucial, for instance,

3 That's already unusual, as Linda Woolverton noted: a Disney heroine who wasn't vain and was into studying. Thus one of the important gifts that the Beast gives Belle is his library.

that Belle's father doesn't pressurize her in the slightest to get married (although he does suggest that Gaston is a handsome enough fellow for Belle to talk to. Once Belle has dismissed Gaston, though, her father does not press her any further – unlike the marquis in *The Beast*, whose overriding goal is to get Mathurin married at whatever cost, even if it means killing his brother). The father-daughter relationship in *Beauty and the Beast*, then, is much farther developed towards proto-feminism (or least anti-boorish patriarchy) than usual in a Disney movie (compare with Jasmine and her father in the following year's *Aladdin*).

Walerian Borowczyk was one of the masters of modern animation, and *Beauty and the Beast* was of course a cel animated movie. However, Borowczyk's working practices were probably completely different from those at Burbank! For instance, 370 people worked on *Beauty and the Beast*, including 43 animators.[4]

Beauty and the Beast looked hugely impressive – particularly the backgrounds and settings: the ballroom, with its candlelit columns against a deep blue starry sky; the warm hues of the village; the gothic exterior of the castle; and the dark castle interiors. This was filmmaking at its very best: *Beauty and the Beast* truly does rank alongside the five 'golden era' films of Disney, as Howard Ashman and the filmmakers wanted it to.[5]

And the animation and characterization of Belle – usually the toughest assignment for animators on a Disney movie – was convincing and forceful. Youth, beauty, resourcefulness (quirkiness), dreams, wistfulness – all the usual requisites of a fairy tale heroine were

---

4 There were 1,040 effects shots, with 10,000 separate elements.

5 Howard Ashman was conscious of making a film that could stand on the shelf next to *Snow White and the Seven Dwarfs* or *Fantasia*. And *Beauty and the Beast* really can do that. Which can't be said of many films regarded by Disney – or marketed by Disney – as 'Disney classics'.

there, but they were believable.

Belle's sisters from Charles Perrault's version of the fairy tale were dropped – instead of the arrogant, jealous sisters (and a bunch of brothers), Belle had Disneyesque sidekicks. Some of those elements from Perrault's tale were transferred to Gaston and his crew (in the fairy tale, suitors for Beauty are mentioned but not named).

French artists such as Jean-Honoré Fragonard were used for inspiration for the *mise-en-scène* of *Beauty and the Beast*: 'his beautiful landscapes, the way he handles trees. When you start these films, you begin with a certain look, then create a style unique to the film', said Lisa Keene, who supervised the backgrounds on *Beauty and the Beast*.[6] You can see examples of Fragonard's paintings and other Rococo and Neo-Baroque images on the walls, and in the design of the furniture. Fragonard is known for his airy, light touch, an art of pale hues and elegant lines (look at the early scenes of *Beauty and the Beast*, in which the animation is pushed to a soft, high key glow).

The layout supervisor on *Beauty and the Beast*, Ed Ghertner, said they tried to use unusual camera angles and staging, to move away from a documentary kind of realism, and also to use theatrical lighting. The effect was operatic and highly theatrical: *Beauty and the Beast* saw a return to the outsize, exaggerated Disneyania of earlier films such as *Snow White and the Seven Dwarfs* and *Fantasia*.

One of the strong points of *Beauty and the Beast* is of course the music (by Alan Menken and Howard Ashman). The film was conceived as a Broadway musical, and the music and the songs were wonderful, doing narrative and dramatic work as well as aesthetic and entertaining work. The stand-out song was 'Beauty and the Beast', sung in the film by Mrs Potts (Angela

6 B. Thomas, 1991, 196.

Lansbury) as Belle and the Beast dance in the ballroom (and reprised over the end titles). It was, rightly, an Oscar-winning song, and the sequence is one of the stand-outs in more recent Disney cinema.

Beauty and the Beast, like *The Little Mermaid* before it, saw a return to the brash, confident Disney picture where the songs carried much of the movie. Films such as *Beauty and the Beast*, and *Aladdin* and *The Hunchback of Notre Dame*, really did bear out a critic's comment that the best Broadway musicals of the time were not in Gotham, but on cinema screens around the world. From *The Little Mermaid* onwards, Disney animations were powered along by terrific musical scores and songs.

BEAUTY AND THE BEASTLA BELLE ET LA BETE

La Belle et la Bête (1945) is a 100% masterpiece of cinema, much admired and much emulated (Tim Burton,[7] Francis Coppola,[8] Dario Argento, Wes Craven, Stanley Kubrick and 100s of other filmmakers have directly quoted it or been influenced by it). Startling, dream-like and self-consciously poetic, *La Belle et la Bête* contains some spell-binding sequences, such as the flying laundry, the arms holding candles, the mirrors (a Cocteau favourite), the costumes, and the Beast smouldering after a kill.

Other versions of *Beauty and the Beast* include movies from 1899, 1903, 1905, 1908, 1912, 1913, 1922,

7 As Tim Burton remarked, all horror films are basically *Beauty and the Beast.*

8 *Beauty and the Beast* was a key reference point for Francis Coppola's 1992 Dracula film in many ways: in the design of the castle, for example (with human arms as candle holders), or in the use of backwards film, or the shots of roses, or Dracula as a beast in the garden with Lucy (*Bram Stoker's Dracula* consciously reworked the fairy tale *Beauty and the Beast*).

1924, 1934, 1952 (dir. Lev Atamanov), 1960, 1961, 1969, 1975, 1976, 1978, 1982, 1983 (dir. Roger Vadim), 1986, 1987, 1992, 1993, 1997, 1998, 2001, 2003, and 2007. A 2009 movie starring Estelle Warren is one of the latest versions.

Of course, 100s of horror movies, fantasy movies, sci-fi movies and the like can be regarded as versions of *Beauty and the Beast.* Some of the obvious ones would include *Dracula, Psycho, Alien, King Kong, Edward Scissorhands, Hallowe'en* and *Phantom of the Opera.*

A NOTE ON FAIRY TALES

The magic of fairy tales continues unabated in the contemporary world, not only for children but for adults too. It is worth noting that Wilhelm and Jacob Grimms' *Children's and Household Tales* is the highest selling book in the West, after the *Bible*, since its publication in the 19th century. Of the key events in the history of the fairy and folk tale, one of the most significant must surely be the publication in 1812 of the Grimm Brothers' stories. They were translated into English by Edgar Taylor and his family (in 1823), and were illustrated by George Cruikshank, one of the great illustrators of the day. It proved to be a brilliant combination of talents (we have re-published the original text of this ground-breaking book).

The typical fairy tale, or the fairy tale as interpreted today, is usually short (3-5 pages long), usually from a Grimm source (perhaps modified by Disney), concentrating on a character who learns how to use magic and gifts to achieve success, and often involves marriage at the end. Women are beautiful, hard-working, and passive; the men are dashing, brave, and adventurous.[9]

It's important to remember, too, that fairy tales today usually mean a narrow range of ten to fifteen stories – always the same ones: *The Frog Prince, Snow White and the Seven Dwarfs, Cinderella, Rapunzel, Sleeping Beauty, Little Red Riding Hood, Hansel and Gretel, Beauty and the Beast, The Pied Piper, The Snow Queen, The Little Mermaid, Bluebeard, Tom Thumb, The Three Little Pigs, The Twelve Dancing Princesses, Jack*

9 J. Zipes, 2000, xxvi.

and the Beanstalk, Puss In Boots, etc.

For Angela Carter, fairy tales are part of folklore, not 'high art', which comes from the proletariat, not the bourgeoisie; in Carter's proto-feminist view (in *The Virago Book of Fairy Tales*), fairy tales speak of spirited, resourceful women, a female character who is 'clever, or brave, or good, or silly, or cruel, or sinister, or awesomely unfortunate' (xiii). Some fairy tales – those of the Grimms and Charles Perrault for example – sometimes punish desire and wildness. In *Little Red Riding Hood*, the protagonist is told not to be adventurous, not to talk to strangers, not to wander from the path. In the work of the Grimms, Hans Christian Andersen and Perrault, one sees the mechanisms of control in a patriarchal world at work – the urge to police desire and adventure, independent thinking and self-liberation. The forbidden is suppressed. Taboos are skirted around, or tackled, unleashing violence and retribution. French feminist Luce Irigaray said in *This Sex Which Is Not One*: 'what is most strictly forbidden to women today is that they should attempt to express their own pleasure'.[10]

FAIRY TALES AND FEMINISM

The following section considers some of the feminist views of fairy tales. From one (modern) viewpoint, fairy tales may be seen as having incidents of inexplicable abuse, maltreatment of women, negative images of minority groups, questionable sacrifices, and the exaltation of power (all of which feature in *The Beast*).[11] Fairy tales offer many opportunities for an identification with the long-suffering protagonist who wins through at the end (as Lucy does, and Romilda does). It is not only the joyous experiences of identification that are celebrated in fairy tales, but also the moments of pain. Suffering

10 *This Sex Which Is Not One*, in L. Irigaray: *The Irigaray Reader*, 125.
11 J. Zipes, 1979, 170; and see R. Moore, 1975.

becomes glamorous, as the poor protagonist reaches new depths of pain and anxiety before winning through.[12] The embattled protagonist is often female, as feminists have noted (Snow White, Rapunzel, Cinderella).

Feminists have long noted the double standards at work in fairy and folk tales, the way women are portrayed as opposites. Women are usually either sweet domestic types or wicked step-mother types. There are many rules and stereotypes: for instance, step-mothers can't be beautiful. Heroines are beautiful, but with beauty comes negative aspects such as passivity and misfortune. Feminists have laid into the passivity of fairy tale heroines, who sit and wait and sit and wait hoping that 'some day my prince will come' (in the *The Beast* the two female protagonists are more active, and have more agency, than the passive heroines of fairy tales). The heroine moves from separation from her natural mother, to the hell of relating to a stepmother, to running away, being outcast, or waiting and musing, to the arrival of the prince and consummation.

The immortal words *once upon a time* herald a movement for the reader/ listener into enchantment and fantasy, but the nuptial rites bring everything back to the domestic, everyday world (the framing story of *The Beast* of course pivots around marriage, but it ends with tragedy and apocalypse). For feminism, these myths become damaging lies. In the view of some feminists, marriage is the endpoint of the fairy tale, and is a claustrophic, repressive initiation into capitalist, bourgeois, heterosexual ideology (that can be seen as taking place in *The Beast*). Marriage is seen in the masculinist system not as the icing on the cake, but the cake itself, the *raison d'être* of the tale. In this view, all points of the

12 M.K. Lieberman: "'Some Day My Prince Will Come'", 1972.

story are driving towards marriage, the romantic, bourgeois, heterosexual nuptial rites of romantic fiction, comicbooks, Mills & Boon novels and TV soap operas. After waiting waiting waiting the reward is marriage: it is an exchange for the heroine of 'one enchanted condition for another'.[13] The happy ever after wedding is the reward for the endeavours of fairy tale heroes and heroines (if *The Beast* was a traditional fairy tale, it would end with Luc/ Romilda and the Mathurin/ beast marrying). It is significant, though, that the fairy tale's endpoint is a party, the wedding, not the long, bitter years of marriage. The wedding seems to 'round off' the story. For other feminists, the marriage and 'happy ever after' of fairy tales is merely something added onto the tale. The arrival of the prince is seen as an unnecessary addition.

The wedding or marriage validates one ideological dimension of fairy stories: the politics of late capitalism, the politics of heterosexual identity, the ideology of patriarchy, and so on. Fairy tales, from Charles Perrault and the Brothers Grimm and hundreds of anonymous sources, are created from a particular late 18th/ early 19th century European socio-political context which puts men and women into particular gender roles. The stereotypes are well known, and feminists have reconsidered them. This's one feminist view; I think that fairy tales are more complex than that, more multi-layered, and more subtle.

As Iona and Peter Opie point out in their excellent collection of fairy tales, most fairy tales *don't* have magic in them. Many have talking animals who act like humans. but far less have magical acts or fairies and witches than one might expect.

The transformations in fairy tales are often not from

13 K.E. Rowe: "Feminism and Fairy Tales", in J. Zipes, 1986, 220.

someone who was morally corrupt or lazy or mean into someone noble and good – embodied in the transformations from peasant to princess, from rags to riches. Rather, the magical transformation is the realization that the hero was *always like that*. In short, it's a *breaking of the spell*. Appearances are deceptive, and fairy tales often wind up with a grand unmasking: the princess turns out to be a nasty sister or impostor; the frog was really a prince. It's the interior, the soul, the heart, that really counts, not the outward appearance.

Another feminist, postmodern or psychoanalytic approach to fairy tales has analyzed the way that looking and seeing is employed (which of course bears directly on cinema, and *The Beast* explores it many times). The visual dimension of fairy tales is something illustrators have obviously taken up, but there is a feminist and postmodern aspect to visual culture, and to seeing in particular, that might be pertinent to a feminist analysis of fairy tales. In the Lacanian psychological model, notions of seeing, pleasure, desire, voyeurism, scopophilia, the mirror stage, the symbolic zone, the phallic realm and the phallus are bound up together. In fairy tales, seeing is not only related to pleasure and desire, but also to death. The sight of all those butchered women in the forbidden room in *Bluebeard*, for example, signals death for the protagonist. And the legend of the l'Esperance creature in the past in *The Beast* begins when Romilda glances out of the window and sees the lamb wandering away. That simple look starts it all off.

CENSORSHIP, VIOLENCE AND FAIRY TALES.

The Beast is an erotic-comic fairy tale in which notions of censorship is foregrounded. With its images of graphic sex and its theme of bestiality, *The Beast* tackles the censorship issue head-on.

Fairy tales are violent, difficult, ambiguous, erotic,

as well as charming, sweet, sentimental and lyrical. But fairy tales were never intended for children: they were always produced by and for adults; only in the later part of the 19th century did the shift towards catering for children occur.

Publishers, teachers, educational boards, broadcasters and filmmakers have all censored fairy tales at one time or another. In *Hansel and Gretel* the witch is pushed into an oven; in *Cinderella* the sisters' eyes are pecked out; in *Little Red Riding Hood* the wolf eats two women; and the witch is made to dance in red-hot shoes in *Snow White and the Seven Dwarfs*.

The violence in fairy tales immediately makes them suspect food for children, who, it is claimed by media pundits, rightwing religious fundamentalists and media watchdogs, copy what they consume in the media. Children, it is claimed, have copied the antics of cartoon characters. If cartoons are violent, then children can become violent.

It is this simplistic argument, this puritanical need to protect children that the some people who love fairy tales detest. It is this form of censorship and policing that destroys works of art. The opposers of censorship (including Walerian Borowczyk) are those of the liberal camp, advocating the sovereignty of notions such as self-expression, and the rights of free speech. It's not so much a question of being right or left wing, republican or democrat, but of minimizing the effects of the mechanisms and institutions of oppression. What the liberal artist doesn't want is someone saying you can do this but not that. The liberal artist must imagine s/he is beyond the dictates of this or that regime or set of laws. S/he must think s/he is free to express themselves as s/he will.

There is, for instance, much spilling of blood in the stories. Fairy and folk stories were not intended to be bloodless. Myths have always had blood spilt in them, and many deaths. Death is part of the overall emotional, spiritual and psychological impact of world mythologies. To erase or soften death in mythology destroys their meaning. When one reads the Brothers Grimm uncensored, one is struck by the violence of the stories, not because the violence is troubling, but because many other versions of fairy and folk tales produced for adults or for children are carefully edited.

Lurking behind every fairy tale is the 'bloody' or 'forbidden chamber', a dark underworld of raw feeling and spiritual power. Behind every fairy tale is the bloody chamber of *Bluebeard,* a place that is at once taboo and fascinating, a place that is both hidden and aching to be revealed (variants in Grimms' tales include *The Robber's Bridegroom* and *Fitcher's Feather Bird*). The temptation story usually involves a woman opening the forbidden chamber, related to the ancient myths of Pandora (and Pandora's box), Psyche, and Orpheus. The bloody chamber is desired and feared. It is a place of love and death. In *The Beast*, both women actively explore sexual desire.

As Sigmund Freud knew well, taboos contain really powerful things. That's why they're taboos (*The Beast* tackles a biggie: inter-species sex). Fairy tales continually present readers with taboos and thresholds: the taboos and thresholds have to be dealt with by the protagonist in the tale. The moralistic aspect of fairy tales is direct: either the protagonist opens the door or doesn't: there is no equivocation, one must choose correctly. The wrong choice is always swiftly punished. The exoteric choices reflect esoteric or inner developments. Sometimes the price to pay for passing a threshold is death, as the women die in *Bluebeard* who cannot resist unlocking the door to the forbidden chamber. Sometimes there is an extraordinary, miraculous reward for the right kind of endeavour.

Bluebeard is in fact a deliciously gruesome tale. Children lap up the horror: there is a thrill in being frightened, as consumers of horror movies and ghost stories know. In *Bluebeard* we hear of a floor which is 'all covered with clotted blood on which lay the bodies of several dead women ranged against the walls' (I. Opie, 38). Bluebeard (sometimes his beard is red; in the Russian *Tsar of the Forest*, it is green), is in fact a serial killer, a mass murderer who joins the ranks of Jack the Ripper, Charles Manson, Ed Gein, the Yorkshire Ripper, and other famous killers. Bluebeard guards a secret room which the protagonist must never enter: it is the same taboo in modern movies such as *Psycho* (1960), where the room no one must enter is Norman Bates' basement. It's characteristic that director Alfred Hitchcock should regard *Psycho* as a comedy, albeit a black comedy (as Walerian Borowczyk did with *La Bête*). Similarly, writers who love fairy tales enjoy their horror, their moments of Gothic atmosphere and coarseness.

SHAPE-SHIFTING.

The figure of the shape-changer is very ancient: the archaic shaman is the model for all deities, magicians, animals and witches who can transform themselves. Wonder tales, oral tales which pre-date literary fairy tales, have *transformation* as one of their foundations, in particular miraculous transformation. As Jack Zipes noted, '[e]verybody and everything can be transformed in a wonder tale'. Usually there was the transformation of the social status of the protagonists (2000, xvii). Mathurin in *The Beast* is part-way shape-shifted, while Lucy, at the end of the picture, naked and clad in a fur coat, is part-beast herself.

Traditionally, shape-shifting means moving from one ontological plane to another: from boy to bird means moving higher up, into transcendence of earthly matters. Being turned by a witch into a frog is clearly a regression to a lower level. The frog is like a primitive, miniature, even caricature version of a human being. For Marie-Louise von Franz the frog as the embodiment of the unconscious is usually aiming to become conscious: it wants to become conscious.[14]

THE BEAST AND *LITTLE RED RIDING HOOD.*

In *Fairy Tales and the Art of Subversion: The Classical Genre for Children and the Process of Civilization*, Jack Zipes sees *Little Red Riding Hood* (*Le Petit Chaperon Rouge* in Charles Perrault, 1697; *Rotkuappchen* (*Little Red Cap*) in the Grimms, 1812), as a patriarchal tale of male power, where a young woman is initiated into the masculinist social world via a rape fantasy (J. Zipes, 1983). For Zipes, there's a 'Little Red Riding Hood syndrome' in Western culture which perverted sexuality in the 18th and 19th centuries and led to 'an instrumentalization of the body', so that (*pace* Michel Foucault) sexuality became a part of the 'development of bio-politics to bring about the supervision of the body as a machine for maximum use and profit'.[15] Seen in this post-Marxist view, *The Beast* is an initiation story, in which Lucy and Romilda are being inducted into the world of patriarchy – as overseen by patriarchal figures such as the marquis, the duke, the Cardinal and others (it's easy to see how Lucy is being traded between aunt Virginia and the marquis, which's how some second wave feminists see marriage – an economic exchange of goods).

For Jack Zipes, the folk tale was originally an oral

14 M. Franz, *The Psychological Meaning of the Redemption Motif in Fairy Tales*, Inner City Books, Toronto, 1980
15 J. Zipes, *The Trials and Tribulations of Little Red Riding Hood*, 46; M. Foucault: *The History of Sexuality*, Pantheon, New York, NY, 1978, 135-9.

narrative form that made sense of life for 'common', working class people. It was not a literary form, but a reflection of their needs and aspirations; it reflected their perception of the moral and social order of the time (1979, 5). In *Don't Bet on the Prince: Contemporary Feminist Fairy Tales in North America and England,* Zipes reckoned that Charles Perrault and the Grimm Brothers had appropriated oral and folk tales and turned them into 'male-cultivated' literary versions (1986, 227). According to Zipes, Perrault made some important changes to the folk tale of *Little Red Riding Hood* when he revised it in 1697: the protagonist became 'spoiled, negligent, and naïve'; she is dressed now in red, colour of sin in Christianity (red is the signature colour in *The Beast*); she speaks to and makes a compact with the wolf; she does pretty much what the wolf wants, and is not clever enough to outwit him.

Wolfishness is associated with sensuality, nature, baseness, animality; the wolf is demonized in the West, becomes associated with the Devil, with witchcraft (lycanthropy), all things 'other' and unknown. The wolf is the sinful 'wild side' of human nature, always to be suppressed; the wolf symbolizes a fear of intercourse and conception (C.G. Jung), or (female) wildness (Sigmund Freud), or racial inferiority (racist German folklorists), depending on which authority one employs.[16]

In *Little Red Riding Hood* a child ventures forth from the domestic, maternal environment into the wide world (from a house to a wild forest). In the tale, the relationship with the mother is pivotal (*The Beast* has the aunt Virginia playing this role): the mother and her maternal power bring back and re-centre the child. In *Little Red Riding Hood* the power of the mother in righting the world is embodied in the promise of good

16 C.G. Jung: *Collected Works*, vol. 4, Rasch, Zurich 1971, 237; see B. Bettelheim, 1976; L. Burns, 1972.

food. At the end of *Little Red Riding Hood* the emphasis shifts from being eaten and pulled out of the wolf's belly to the mother again providing food and wine for the grandmother in Little Red Cap's next trip into the now-secure forest.

In *Little Red Riding Hood* the gender of the girl and the wolf is significant: the wolf stands for, unsubtly, the strange men mothers warn their children about. Feminists such as Angela Carter, Catherine Storr, the Merseyside Fairy Story Collective, O.F. Gmelin, Margaret Kassajep and Tanith Lee have used the wolf or wolfishness as a metaphor for proud female sensuality (one could cite Lucy in her fur coat as a bold image of empowerment). The wolf is associated, in traditional symbolism and mythology, with Mother Goddesses, motherhood and fecundity. In Jack Zipes' feminist reading, Charles Perrault turned *Little Red Riding Hood* into a Christian morality tale about the sinfulness of sex (this is a theme in *The Beast*). The sexual content of the young woman's encounter with the wolf was sanitized by Charles Perrault and the Grimms, but subsequent writers have, Zipes maintains, been attracted to the sexual undercurrent in the tale. The rape aspect of *Little Red Riding Hood* is too explosive for most critics to deal with – they shun it, as they shun problems of rape in Thomas Hardy's *Tess of the d'Urbervilles* (which mirrors *Little Red Riding Hood* in Tess's encounter with Alec in the dark forest). *The Beast* confronts the rape fantasy head-on.

Second wave (1970s and 1980s) feminists such as Andrea Dworkin, Kate Millett and Susan Brownmiller were quick to seize on fairy tales as expressions of male power and patriarchal views of sexuality. In *Men, Women and Rape,* Brownmiller states baldly: '*Little Red*

Riding Hood is a parable of rape'.[17] For radical second wave feminists, the lessons to be learnt from *Little Red Riding Hood* are: watch out, men are lurking in the woods/ world, waiting to rape the unsuspecting woman. Of course, in walking alone into the forest, Red Riding Hood is 'asking for it', one of the commonest male defences of rape.

In the Grimm Brothers' version, the young woman is warned by her mother about not straying from the straight and narrow path. The horror of the story is made good by the arrival of the woodcutter or father figure, who saves the 'girl from herself and her lustful desires.'[18] The young woman cannot manage on her own. Women cannot get by without men and male protection. The man comes in to complete the story, right at the end, as in *Snow White and the Seven Dwarfs* and *Rapunzel.*

The Grimms' *Little Red Cap* reinforced the emphasis on moral duty: the instructions of the girl's mother are crucial: one must walk along the straight and narrow path and not deviate from it for even a moment, and certainly not for pleasures such as flower-picking or dallying with strangers. In the Grimms' version of *Little Red Riding Hood,* the forest is a realm of delights which must be avoided. If indulged, there must be a cost, and a punishment.

> They [the Grimms] eliminated the cruelty and sexuality from the tale, demanded that the child repress her own sensuality, and obligated her to meet the normative standards of responsibility set by adults [remarked Jack Zipes in *Fairy Tales and the Art of Subversion*]. Little Red Cap was compelled to become eminently rational in her anti-climactic adventure. (1983, 16)

17 S. Brownmiller: *Men, Women and Rape* Bantham, New York, 1976, 344.
18 J. Zipes, 1983, 230.

The *Little Red Riding Hood* story can be seen as a quest for self-realization or identity. Going into the forest is one of the primary stages in the mythic quest. Red Riding Hood comes face to face with otherness or strangeness, and, significantly, that otherness, the wolf, is framed in sexual terms. In patriarchal terms, to 'become a woman' means not initiations such as menstruation in puberty but sexual intercourse.

An Andrea Dworkinian reading of *Little Red Riding Hood* would see the overt sexualization of the young woman as part of masculinist/ patriarchal notions of initiation and identity. That is, Red Riding Hood is not a 'real woman' until she's had sex (Lucy Broadhurst in *The Beast* is meant to be a virgin). These are the experiences or meanings that fairy tale illustrators cannot show but can only suggest (as in Gustave Doré's 1862 pictures for Charles Perrault's version). In Jack Zipes' view, other readings of *Little Red Riding Hood* which ignore the potent erotic subtext are invalid. In *The Uses of Enchantment: The Meaning and Importance of Fairy Tales,* Bruno Bettelheim sees the tale as a Freudian struggle between conflicting commands from the super-ego and ego, an œdipal tension to do with following and subverting parental laws.[19]

19 B. Bettelheim, 1976, 181.

FILMOGRAPHY

FILMS DIRECTED BY WALERIAN BOROWCZYK

La Bête (1975)
A.k.a. *The Beast in Heat. The Beast. Death's Ecstasy*

CAST

Sirpa Lane - Romilda de l'Esperance.
Lisbeth Hummel - Lucy Broadhurst.
Elisabeth Kaza - Virginia Broadhurst.
Pierre Benedetti - Mathurin de l'Esperance.
Guy Tréjan - Pierre de l'Esperance.
Roland Armontel - Priest.
Marcel Dalio - Duc De Balo.
Pascale Rivault - Clarisse De l'Esperance.
Hassane Fall - Ifany.
Anna Baldaccini - Théodore.
Thierry Bourdon - Modeste.
Marie Testanière - Marie.
Stéphane Testanière - Stéphane.
Mathieu Rivollier.
Julien Hanany.
Robert Capia.

CREW

Producer - Anatole Dauman
Script - Walerian Borowczyk
Cinematography - Bernard Daillencourt, Marcel Grignon
Music - Domenico Scarlatti
Editing - Walerian Borowczyk

Production Design – Jacques D'Ovidio
Set Decoration – Alain Guillé
Costume Design – Piet Bolscher
Makeup – Odette Berroyer
Production Manager – Dominique Duvergé
Sound – Michel Laurent, Alex Pront, Jean-Pierre Ruh
Camera operator – Gérard Wurtz
Editorial – Florence Bory
Assistant editors – Alain Cayrade, Florence Dauman, Claude Delon, Jean-Pierre Platel, Monique Prim, Michel Valio

OTHER MOVIES DIRECTED BY WALERIAN BOROWCZYK

Goto, Island of Love (1968) A.k.a. *Goto, l'île d'amour*
Producers – Louis Duchesne, René Thévenet
Script – Walerian Borowczyk, Dominique Duvergé

Blanche (1971)
Producer – Philippe d'Argila, Dominique Duvergé
Script – Walerian Borowczyk

Immoral Tales (1974) A.k.a. *Contes Immoraux*
Producer – Anatole Dauman
Script – Walerian Borowczyk, André Pieyre de Mandiargues

Story of Sin (1975)
Script – Walerian Borowczyk

La Marge (1976)
A.k.a. *Emmanuelle '77. The Margin. The Streetwalker*
Producer – Raymond and Robert Hakim
Script – Walerian Borowczyk

Behind Convent Walls (1977)
A.k.a. *Interno di un convento. Sex Life in a Convent. Within a Cloister*
Producer – Giuseppe Vezzani
Script – Walerian Borowczyk

Three Immoral Women (1979)
A.k.a. *Heroines of Evil. Heroines of Pain. Immoral Women*

Producers - Pierre Braunberger and Gisèle Braun-berger
Executive producers - Jean-Paul De Vidas, Michel de Vidas
Script - Walerian Borowczyk, story - André Pieyre de Mandiargues

Lulu (1980)
Producers - Robert Kuperberg, Jean-Pierre Labrande
Script - Walerian Borowczyk, Anton Giulio Majano, Géza von Radványi

Doctor Jeckyll and His Women (1981)
A.k.a. *Docteur Jekyll et les femmes. The Blood/bath of Doctor Jeckyll. Bloodlust. Dr. Jeckyll and Miss Osbourne. The Experiment*
Producers - Ralph Baum, Robert Kuperberg, Jean-Pierre Labrande
Script - Walerian Borowczyk, from Robert Louis Stevenson's novel *The Strange Case of Dr. Jeckyll and Mr. Hyde*

The Art of Love (1983)
A.k.a. *Ars Amandi. L'arte di amare. L'Art d'aimer*
Producers - Marcel Albertini, Jacques Nahum, Ugo Tucci
Script - Walerian Borowczyk, Wilhelm Buchheim, Enzo Ungari

Emmanuelle 5 (1987)
Producer - Alain Siritzky
Script - Walerian Borowczyk and Alex Cunningham

Love Rites (1988)
A.k.a. *Cérémonie d'amour. Queen of the Night. Rites of Love*
Producer - Alain Sarde, Philippe Guez
Script - Walerian Borowczyk, from André Pieyre de Mandiargues' novel *Tout disparaitra*

OTHER FILM PROJECTS DIRECTED BY WALERIAN BOROWCZYK

Mois d'août (1946)
Photographies vivantes (1954)
Atelier de Fernand Léger (1954)

Autumn (a.k.a. Jesien, 1955)
Once Upon a Time (1957)
School (1958)
Requited Feelings (a.k.a. Nagrodzone uczucia, 1958)
Dom (1959)
Les astronautes (1959)
Le concert de M. et Mme. Kabal (1962)
L'encyclopedie de grand-maman en 13 volumes (1963)
Holy Smoke (1963)
Renaissance (1964)
Les jeux des anges (1965)
Le dictionnaire de Joachim (1965)
Rosalie (1966)
Diptyque (1967)
Mr. and Mrs. Kabal's Theatre (a.k.a. Théâtre de M. et Mme. Kabal, 1967)
Gavotte (1968)
Le phonographe (1969)
Une collection particulière (1973)
Brief von Paris (1975)
Escargot de Venus (1975)
L'amour monstre de tous les temps (1977)
Private Collections (1979), segment: L'armoire
Scherzo infernal (1984)
Série rose (a.k.a. Softly from Paris, 4 episodes, 1986-1991)
  Le lotus d'or (1986)
  Un traitement mérité (1990)
  Almanach des adresses des demoiselles de Paris (1990)
  L'experte Halima (1991)

BIBLIOGRAPHY

Sue Adler. "Enticements to Voyeurism", *Cinema Papers*, 50, Feb, 1985

B. Bettelheim: *The Uses of Enchantment: The Meaning and Importance of Fairy Tales*, Knopf, New York, 1976

W. Borowczyk. *Anatomy of the Devil*, 1992

–. *My Polish Years*, Hypnos Media, Paris, 2001

Borowczyk: Cinéaste Onirique: Le cas étrange du Dr Jekyll et Miss Osbourne, Collection La Vue and B. Diffusion, Paris, 1981

A. Carter: *The Virago Book of Fairy Tales*, Virago 1991

D.A. Cook. *A History of Narrative Film*, W.W. Norton, New York, NY, 1981, 1990, 1996

J. Gerber. *Anatole Dauman: Pictures of a Producer*, British Film Institute, London, 1992

T. Gilliam. *Gilliam on Gilliam*, ed. I. Christie, Faber, London, 1999

L. Irigaray: *The Irigaray Reader*, ed. M. Whitford, Blackwell, Oxford, 1991

S. Jaworzy, ed. *Shock: The Essential Guide to Exploitation Cinema*, Titan Books, London, 1996

C. Kessler. "How You Look at It: The Beastly Art of Walerian Borowczyk", in *Video Watchdog*, Special Edition, 1

–. *Cinema Papers*, 128, 129

Elaine Marks & Isabelle de Courtivron, eds. *New French Feminisms: an Anthology*, Harvester Wheatsheaf, 1981

Tom Milne. "Héroïnes du mal, Les (Three Immoral Women)", *Monthly Film Bulletin*, July 1981

K. Newman. *Nightmare Movies*, Harmony, New York, NY, 1988

I. & P. Opie: *The Classic Fairy Tales*, Paladin, 1980

M. Praz. *The Romantic Agony*, tr. Davidson, Oxford University Press, Oxford, 1933

M. Richardson. *Surrealism and Cinema*, Berg, New York, NY, 2006

B. Thomas. *Disney's Art of Animation From Mickey Mouse to*

Beauty and the Beast, Hyperion, New York, NY, 1991
D. Thomson. "That Hairy Monster" [on Walerian Borowczyk's *The Beast*], *Sight & Sound*, June, 2001
C. Tohill & P. Tombs. *Immoral Tales: Sex and Horror Cinema in Europe 1956-1984*, Titan Books, London, 1995
P. Verlaine. *Selected Poems*, tr. J. Richardson, Penguin, London, 1974
Walerian Borowczyk di Valerio Caprara, La Nuova Italia, Florence, 1981
M. Warner. *From the Beast to the Blonde: On Fairy Tales and Their Tellers*, Vintage, London, 1995
J. Zipes. *Breaking the Spell: Radical Theories of Folk and Fairy Tales*, Heinemann, London, 1978
–. "Who's Afraid of the Brothers Grimm? Socialization and Politicization through Fairy Tales", *Lion and the Unicorn*, 3, Winter, 1979-80
–. *Fairy Tales and the Art of Subversion: The Classical Genre for Children and the Process of Civilization*, Heinemann, London, 1983
–. *Trials and Tribulations of Little Red Riding Hood: Versions of the Tale in Socio-Cultural Context*, Heinemann, London, 1983
–. *Don't Bet on the Prince: Contemporary Feminist Fairy Tales in North America and England*, Methuen, New York, NY, 1986
–. "The Enchanted Forest of the Brothers Grimm: New Modes of Approaching the Grimms' Fairy Tales", *Germanic Review*, 62, 1987
–. *The Brothers Grimm: From Enchanted Forests to the Modern World*, Routledge, New York, NY, 1989
–. ed. *The Oxford Companion To Fairy Tales*, Oxford University Press, 2000
–. *Sticks and Stones: The Troublesome Success of Children's Literature From Slovenly Peter to Harry Potter*, Routledge, London, 2002
–. *The Enchanted Screen: The Unknown History of Fairy-tale Films*, Routledge, New York, NY, 2011
–. *The Irresistible Fairy Tale*, Prince University Press, Princeton, NJ, 2012

Jeremy Robinson has written many critical studies, including *Hayao Miyazaki, Walerian Borowczyk, Arthur Rimbaud*, and *The Sacred Cinema of Andrei Tarkovsky*, plus literary monographs on: William Shakespeare; Samuel Beckett; Thomas Hardy; André Gide; Robert Graves; and John Cowper Powys.

It's amazing for me to see my work treated with such passion and respect. There is nothing resembling it in the U.S. in relation to my work.
Andrea Dworkin (on *Andrea Dworkin*)

This model monograph – it is an exemplary job, and I'm very proud that he has accorded me a couple of mentions... The subject matter of his book is beautifully organised and dead on beam.
Lawrence Durrell (on *The Light Eternal: A Study of J.M.W. Turner*)

His poetry is very good deep moving stuff.
Cloud Nine magazine

Jeremy Robinson's poetry is certainly jammed with ideas, and I find it very interesting for that reason. It's certainly a strong imprint of his personality.
Colin Wilson

Sex-Magic-Poetry-Cornwall is a very rich essay... It is a very good piece... vastly stimulating and insightful.
Peter Redgrove

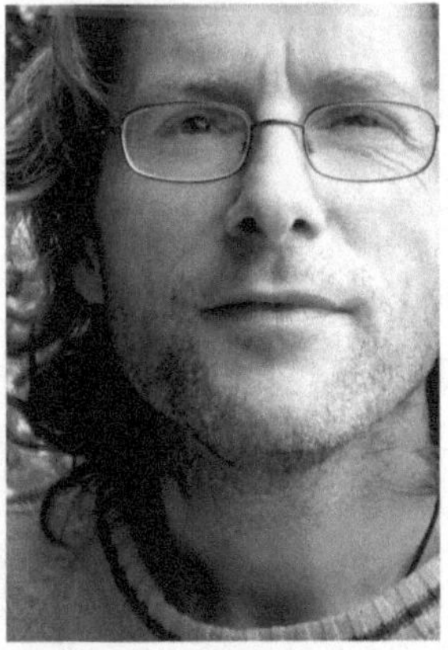

ARTS, PAINTING, SCULPTURE

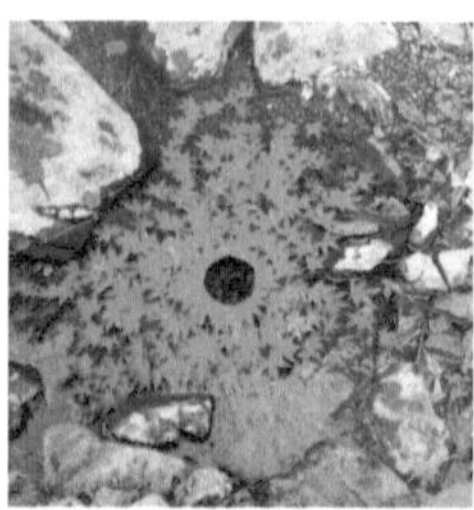

The Art of Andy Goldsworthy
Andy Goldsworthy: Touching Nature
Andy Goldsworthy in Close-Up
Andy Goldsworthy: Pocket Guide
Andy Goldsworthy In America
Land Art: A Complete Guide
The Art of Richard Long
Richard Long: Pocket Guide
Land Art In Great Britain
Land Art in Close-Up
Land Art In the U.S.A.
Land Art: Pocket Guide
Installation Art in Close-Up

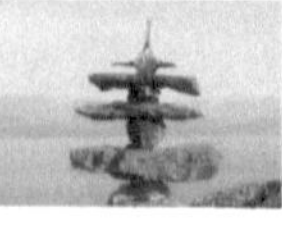

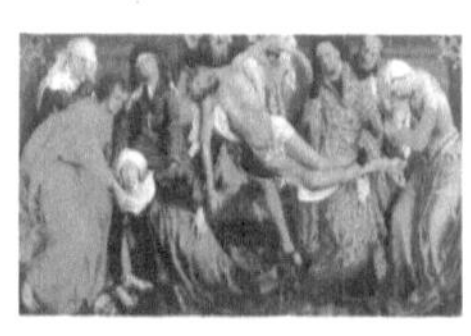

Minimal Art and Artists In the 1960s and After
Colourfield Painting
Land Art DVD, TV documentary
Andy Goldsworthy DVD, TV documentary
The Erotic Object: Sexuality in Sculpture From Prehistory to the Present Day
Sex in Art: Pornography and Pleasure in Painting and Sculpture
Postwar Art
Sacred Gardens: The Garden in Myth, Religion and Art
Glorification: Religious Abstraction in Renaissance and 20th Century Art
Early Netherlandish Painting
Jasper Johns
Brice MardenLeonardo da Vinci
Piero della Francesca
Giovanni Bellini

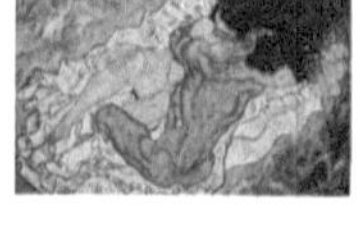

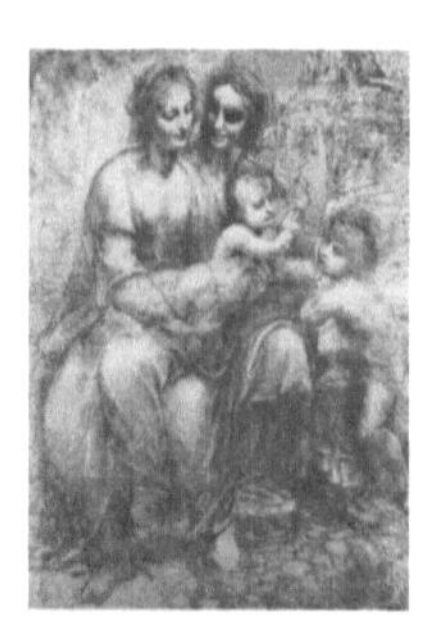

Fra Angelico: Art and Religion in the Renaissance
Mark Rothko: The Art of Transcendence
Frank Stella: American Abstract Artist
Alison Wilding: The Embrace of Sculpture
Vincent van Gogh: Visionary Landscapes
Eric Gill: Nuptials of God
Constantin Brancusi: Sculpting the Essence of Things
Max Beckmann
Gustave Moreau
Caravaggio
Egon Schiele: Sex and Death In Purple Stockings
Delizioso Fotografico Fervore: Works In Process 1
Sacro Cuore: Works In Process 2
The Light Eternal: J.M.W. Turner
The Madonna Glorified: Karen Arthurs

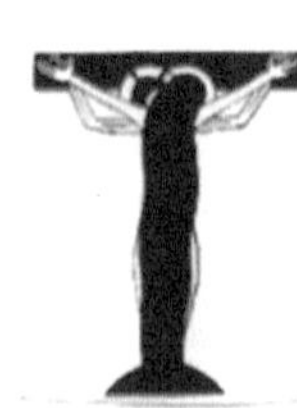

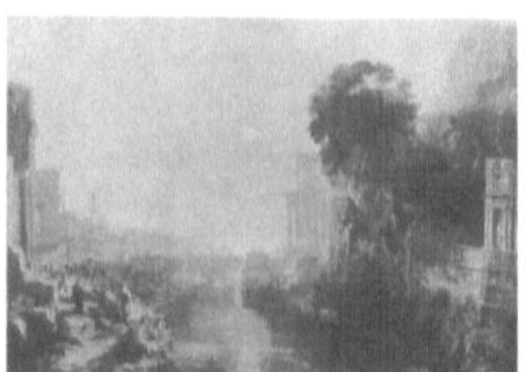

LITERATURE

J.R.R. Tolkien: The Books, The Films, The Whole Cultural Phenomenon
J.R.R. Tolkien: Pocket Guide
Beauties, Beasts and Enchantment: Classic French Fairy Tales
Tolkien's Heroic Quest
Brothers Grimm: German Popular Stories
Sexing Hardy: Thomas Hardy and Feminism
Thomas Hardy's *Tess of the d'Urbervilles*
Thomas Hardy's *Jude the Obscure*
Thomas Hardy: The Tragic Novels
Love and Tragedy: Thomas Hardy
The Poetry of Landscape in Hardy
Wessex Revisited: Thomas Hardy and John Cowper Powys
Wolfgang Iser: Essays and Interviews
Petrarch, Dante and the Troubadours
Maurice Sendak and the Art of Children's Book Illustration
Andrea Dworkin
Cixous, Irigaray, Kristeva: The *Jouissance* of French Feminism
Julia Kristeva: Art, Love, Melancholy, Philosophy, Semiotics and Psychoanalysis
Hélene Cixous I Love You: The *Jouissance* of Writing
Luce Irigaray: Lips, Kissing, and the Politics of Sexual Difference
Peter Redgrove: Here Comes the Flood
Peter Redgrove: Sex-Magic-Poetry-Cornwall
Lawrence Durrell: Between Love and Death, East and West
Love, Culture & Poetry: Lawrence Durrell
Cavafy: Anatomy of a Soul
German Romantic Poetry: Goethe, Novalis, Heine, Hölderlin
Novalis: *Hymns To the Night*
Feminism and Shakespeare
Shakespeare: *The Sonnets*
Shakespeare: Love, Poetry & Magic
The Passion of D.H. Lawrence
D.H. Lawrence: Symbolic Landscapes
D.H. Lawrence: Infinite Sensual Violence
The Ecstasies of John Cowper Powys
Sensualism and Mythology: The Wessex Novels of John Cowper Powys
Amorous Life: John Cowper Powys (H.W. Fawkner)
Postmodern Powys: New Essays on John Cowper Powys (Joe Boulter)
Rethinking Powys: Critical Essays on John Cowper Powys
Paul Bowles & Bernardo Bertolucci
Rainer Maria Rilke
Joseph Conrad: *Heart of Darkness*
In the Dim Void: Samuel Beckett
Samuel Beckett Goes into the Silence
André Gide: Fiction and Fervour
Jackie Collins and the Blockbuster Novel
Blinded By Her Light: The Love-Poetry of Robert Graves

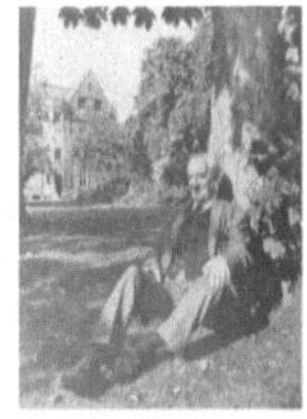
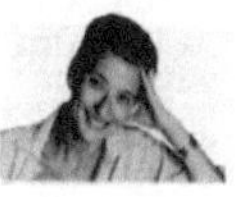
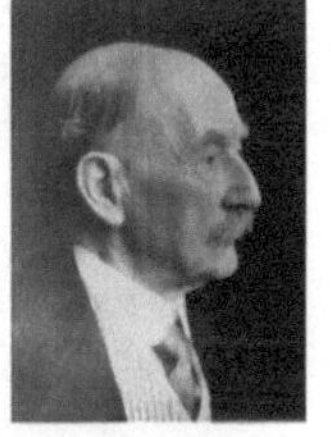
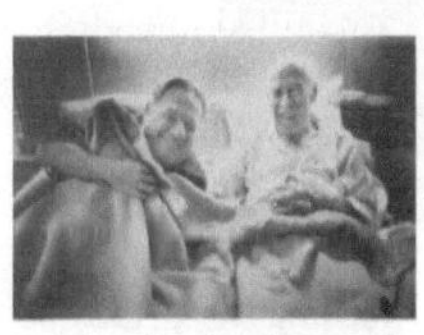
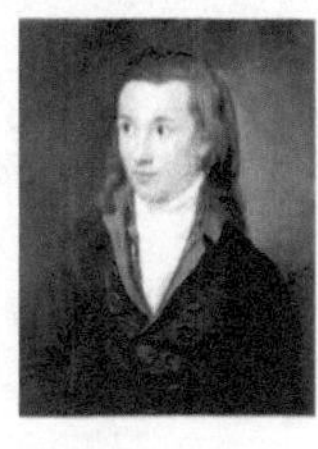

POETRY

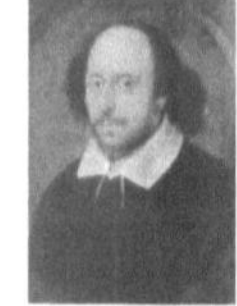
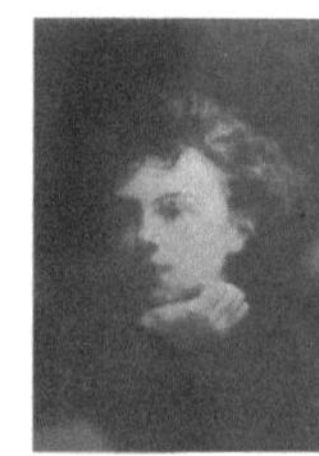

Ursula Le Guin: *Walking In Cornwall*
Peter Redgrove: Here Comes The Flood
Peter Redgrove: Sex-Magic-Poetry-Cornwall
Dante: Selections From the *Vita Nuova*
Petrarch, Dante and the Troubadours
William Shakespeare: *The Sonnets*
William Shakespeare: Complete Poems
Blinded By Her Light: The Love-Poetry of Robert Graves
Emily Dickinson: Selected Poems
Emily Brontë: Poems
Thomas Hardy: Selected Poems
Percy Bysshe Shelley: Poems
John Keats: Selected Poems
John Keats: Poems of 1820
D.H. Lawrence: Selected Poems
Edmund Spenser: Poems
Edmund Spenser: *Amoretti*
John Donne: Poems
Henry Vaughan: Poems
Sir Thomas Wyatt: Poems
Robert Herrick: Selected Poems
Rilke: Space, Essence and Angels in the Poetry of Rainer Maria Rilke
Rainer Maria Rilke: Selected Poems
Friedrich Hölderlin: Selected Poems
Arseny Tarkovsky: Selected Poems
Paul Verlaine: Selected Poems
Novalis: *Hymns To the Night*
Arthur Rimbaud: Selected Poems
Arthur Rimbaud: *A Season in Hell*
Arthur Rimbaud and the Magic of Poetry
D.J. Enright: By-Blows
Jeremy Reed: *Brigitte's Blue Heart*
Jeremy Reed: *Claudia Schiffer's Red Shoes*
Gorgeous Little Orpheus
Radiance: New Poems
Crescent Moon Book of Nature Poetry
Crescent Moon Book of Love Poetry
Crescent Moon Book of Mystical Poetry
Crescent Moon Book of Elizabethan Love Poetry
Crescent Moon Book of Metaphysical Poetry
Crescent Moon Book of Romantic Poetry
Pagan America: New American Poetry

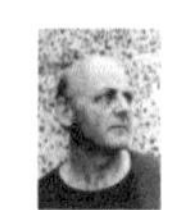
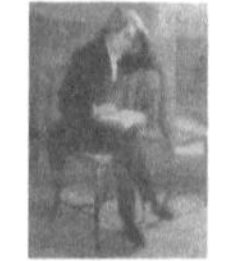
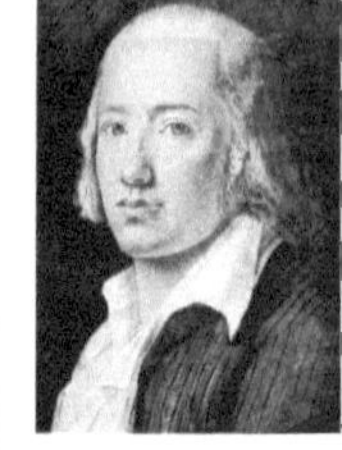
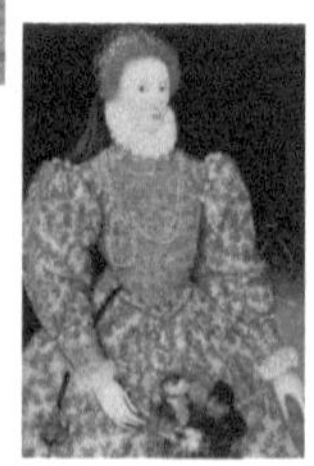

MEDIA, CINEMA, FEMINISM and CULTURAL STUDIES

J.R.R. Tolkien: The Books, The Films, The Whole Cultural Phenomenon
J.R.R. Tolkien: Pocket Guide
The *Lord of the Rings* Movies: Pocket Guide
The Ghost Dance: The Origins of Religion
The Cinema of Hayao Miyazaki
Hayao Miyazaki: *Princess Mononoke*: Pocket Movie Guide
Hayao Miyazaki: *Spirited Away*: Pocket Movie Guide
The Peyote Cult

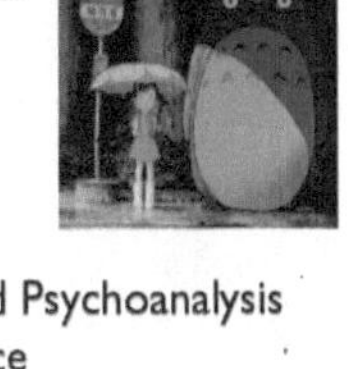

Cixous, Irigaray, Kristeva: The *Jouissance* of French Feminism
Julia Kristeva: Art, Love, Melancholy, Philosophy, Semiotics and Psychoanalysis
Luce Irigaray: Lips, Kissing, and the Politics of Sexual Difference
Hélene Cixous I Love You: The *Jouissance* of Writing
Andrea Dworkin
'Cosmo Woman': The World of Women's Magazines
Women in Pop Music

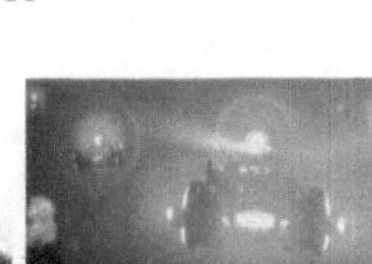

Discovering the Goddess (Geoffrey Ashe)
The Poetry of Cinema
The Sacred Cinema of Andrei Tarkovsky
Andrei Tarkovsky: Pocket Guide
Andrei Tarkovsky: *Mirror*: Pocket Movie Guide
Walerian Borowczyk: Cinema of Erotic Dreams
Jean-Luc Godard: The Passion of Cinema
Jean-Luc Godard: Pocket Guide

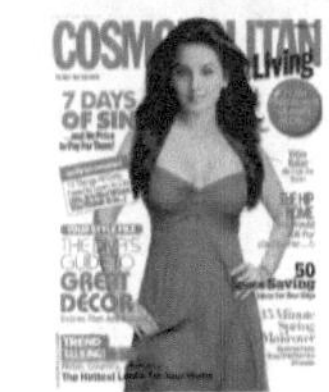

John Hughes and Eighties Cinema
Ferris Buller's Day Off: Pocket Movie Guide
The Cinema of Richard Linklater
Liv Tyler: Star In Ascendance
Blade Runner and the Films of Philip K. Dick
Paul Bowles and Bernardo Bertolucci
Media Hell: Radio, TV and the Press
Detonation Britain: Nuclear War in the UK
Feminism and Shakespeare

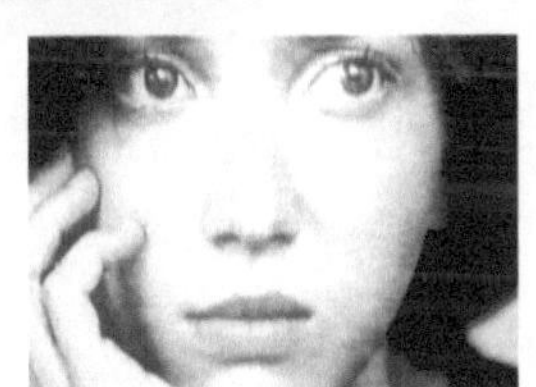

Wild Zones: Pornography, Art and Feminism
Sex in Art: Pornography and Pleasure in Painting and Sculpture
Sexing Hardy: Thomas Hardy and Feminism

The Light Eternal is a model monograph, an exemplary job. The subject matter of the book is beautifully organised and dead on beam. (Lawrence Durrell)

It is amazing for me to see my work treated with such passion and respect. (Andrea Dworkin)

Sex-Magic-Poetry-Cornwall is a very rich essay... It is like a brightly-lighted box. (Peter Redgrove)

CRESCENT MOON PUBLISHING P.O. Box 1312, Maidstone, Kent, ME14 5XU, England
0044-1622-729593 cresmopub@yahoo.co.uk www.crmoon.com

www.ingramcontent.com/pod-product-compliance
Lightning Source LLC
LaVergne TN
LVHW051000080826
845145LV00009B/2387

* 9 7 8 1 8 6 1 7 1 4 2 4 4 *